Pearson Scott Foresman
Writing Rubrics and Anchor Papers

Glenview, Illinois
Boston, Massachusetts
Chandler, Arizona
Upper Saddle River, New Jersey

ISBN-13: 978-0-328-47657-2
ISBN-10:   0-328-47657-9

6 7 8 9 10 V031 15 14 13 12

Contents

Support for Writing

Suggestions for Using This Book

This book is most effective when used in conjunction with the weekly writing lessons and unit writing process lessons in Scott Foresman's *Reading Street.* Rubrics and anchor papers can be copied and distributed or made into transparencies. Here are some ways to use the materials.

- Distribute copies of page v to students. Work through the explanations of traits with the class to develop background for discussing scores.

- Display one-by-one the four models for a given mode in order (starting with Score 1 or Score 4). Work through the commentaries that appear along with the models to illustrate how each got its score.

- After students become proficient with determining scores, distribute copies of writing models from this book with the scores screened out. Work with students to arrive at scores.

- Display a model that is Score 1. Work with students to improve the model.

- Display the rubric for the type of writing you are teaching. Have students use the rubric to evaluate their own writing.

- Distribute copies of the Self-Evaluation Guide on page vi. Have students use this guide to evaluate their work.

Tips for Teaching and Evaluating Writing

- Choose one writing trait to emphasize each week. Appoint a team of students for each trait. Have them find their trait in selections they read and in their own writing and present their findings to the class.

- Read short passages from literature (for example, a tall tale) and from other content areas (for example, a science text). Point out how writer's purpose determines voice, word choice, and style.

- Remember that a writer may be more proficient in one trait than in another. To arrive at a score, evaluators must weigh proficiency in all traits.

- Tell students that when they evaluate their own writing, assigning a score of 3, 2, or even 1 does not necessarily indicate a failure. The ability to identify areas for improvement in future writing is a valuable skill.

- Encourage students to think of themselves as writers. Alert them that subjects, words, and ideas are everywhere. Suggest they keep a notebook handy to record material, such as overheard conversations, sentences from their reading, and vivid words they encounter.

- Join students as they write. Share your own writing with them and ask for their feedback on your work.

- Model constructive ways of giving feedback on writing. *(Words such as* pounce *and* swat *give me a good picture of your cat. You said her name is Boots. How did she get that name? You mentioned that she has a favorite place to sleep. Could you describe it?)*

Traits

- Focus/Ideas
- Organization
- Voice
- Word Choice
- Sentences
- Conventions

- **Focus/Ideas** refers to the main purpose for writing and the details that make the subject clear and interesting. It includes development of ideas through support and elaboration.

- **Organization** refers to the overall structure that guides readers through a piece of writing. Within that structure, transitions show how ideas, sentences, and paragraphs are connected.

- **Voice** shows the writer's unique personality and establishes a connection between writer and reader. Voice, which contributes to style, should be suited to the audience and the purpose for writing.

- **Word Choice** is the use of precise, vivid words to communicate effectively and naturally. It helps create style through the use of specific nouns, lively verbs and adjectives, and accurate, well-placed modifiers.

- **Sentences** covers strong, well-built sentences that vary in length and type. Skillfully written sentences have pleasing rhythms and flow fluently.

- **Conventions** refers to mechanical correctness and includes grammar, usage, spelling, punctuation, capitalization, and paragraphing.

Self-Evaluation Guide

Name ____

Name of Writing Product _______________________________

Directions Review your final draft. Then rate yourself on a scale from 4 to 1 (4 is a top score) on each writing trait. After you fill out the chart, answer the questions.

Writing Traits	4	3	2	1
Focus/Ideas				
Organization				
Voice				
Word Choice				
Sentences				
Conventions				

1. What is the best part of this piece of writing? Why do you think so?

____

____

____

2. Write one thing you would change about this piece of writing if you had the chance to write it again.

____

____

____

Writing Models

Think about a friend, relative, or pet you care about and feel loyalty toward. Write a personal narrative about an incident that shows you cared or were cared for.

Rubric	4	3	2	1
Focus/Ideas	Personal narrative well focused, many supporting details	Personal narrative well focused, some supporting details	Personal narrative often off topic; few supporting details	Personal narrative without focus or sufficient details
Organization	Clear sequence of events with time-order words	Reasonably clear sequence with one or two lapses	Confused sequence of events	No attempt to put events in sequence
Voice	Sincere, engaging voice; feelings clear	Pleasant voice but not compelling or unique	No clear, original voice	Flat writing; no identifiable
Word Choice	Vivid words that show instead of tell	Some vivid words that show instead of tell	Few vivid words that show instead of tell	No attempt to show instead of tell
Sentences	Clear sentences; variety of sentence types	Mostly clear sentences with some variety	Some sentences unclear; little variety	Incomplete or run-on sentences
Conventions	Few, if any, errors	Several minor errors	Many errors that detract from writing	Numerous errors that prevent understanding

Me, My Dad, and My Broken Leg

I broke my leg when I was nine years old. I was swinging on my tire swing when suddenly the rope came loose. I soared through the clear, blue, sky. I hit the cold, hard ground. My dad heard my piercing cries and rushed me to the hospital. In the car he told jokes. "Wait until I get home," he said. "That swing is grounded for a month!" I couldn't help but laugh.

When we arrived at the hospital, Dad carefully scooped up my trembling body and carried me inside. As we waited for the doctor, I squeezed Dad's hand. He squeezed back gently and winked. The doctor came in and explained that she had to straighten my twisted leg before she could set it in a cast. My stomach dropped. Suddenly, Dad yelled, "Wow!" I whipped my head around to see what was happening. Dad said, "Done!" and smiled. I looked back at my leg. It was straight, and the doctor was already preparing the cast.

Continued on next page

> Finally, it was time to go home. I didn't know how to use my new crutches, and I was afraid of looking foolish. So you know what Dad did? He asked the nurse if he could have some crutches too! Together we fumbled and zig-zagged our way to the car.
>
> My dad has always supported me, but on that day he was there when I needed him most. His humor and care helped me through a painful and scary experience. If my dad ever needs me, I know I'll be there for him too.

Score 4

This narrative captures a special event and expresses the writer's feelings about it. Voice is earnest and appealing. Word choice is precise. Sentences are varied and clear. There is good control of conventions.

My Mom

There are many people in my life that I am close to, but my mom has really done a lot for me. She has helped me more times in my life than I can count, but there is one special time I will always remember.

One day when I was at school, my friends stopped talking to me. I tried to ask them what happened. But they wouldn't say anything. It really upset me because they were my best friends. The four of us went places together, like the movies, shopping, and just hanging out. We always told each other everything, and we always tried to make each other feel better when we were sad. So I didn't understand why they would treat me like I wasn't their friend anymore. I was very upset that day, and all I wanted to do was go home.

When I got home that afternoon, I told my mom what had happened, and I got sad and started to cry. I didn't know what I had done to make my friends act that way, and I was very disappointed. My mom took the time to listen to my story. She gave me a warm, comforting hug

Continued on next page

and told me that if they were acting like that, they weren't my real friends in the first place. She told me that I should ignore them and focus on what I'm doing and to make sure that I did the right thing.

My mom helped me feel better and gave me great advise that worked. I know that if I have a problem, I can ask my mom and she will know what to do, because she has gone through similar problems. That was a time in my life when a relative that I feel loyalty toward has cared for me.

Score 3

Narrative is well focused on a single event and includes a number of supporting details. The writer makes smooth transitions from one paragraph to the next. The writer's voice is pleasant and her feelings about the situation and her mother are evident. Sentences are mostly clear and varied. There is a fragment in the second paragraph and a misspelled word in the first sentence of the final paragraph.

Indy

Indy is my aunt's dog that she adopted last Chrismas. After a few months, everybody has definitley grown fond of him. Because I don't have a dog, or any other pet for that matter, Indy is the closest thing that I have to a pet. He is definitley like my pet because I see him almost every Sunday. I always play with him and take him to dog parks and play with a ball. He is loyal to me because he is always there when none of my cousins are at Grandmas house and I have no one to hang out with. I am loyal to him because I always play with him when he is lonley. He used to bark a lot when no one would play. I thought it was a mean bark and I would get scarred. Now, I know that when he barks, he just wants to play. I play with him and he stops barking. Sometimes when my aunt is going out of town, we get to baby-sit Indy and that is when he gets the most playtime. Most of the day when my aunt is at work, Indy is in his cage, but when we watch him, he isn't in his cage as long and he gets to play more. I take him on walks, even when

Continued on next page

I'm busy, to take care of him because I love him. In a big way, Indy is like my own dog and I care for him. That is why I think Indy is one of the most loyal animals in the whole world.

Score 2

This narrative does not appropriately address the prompt. The writer doesn't focus on any particular incident in which she took care of her aunt's dog, but rather addresses their relationship in general. Because of this there is no clear sequence of events. Voice is evident and pleasant. Sentences are generally varied, though many begin with *I* or *He*. There are a number of punctuation and spelling errors that detract from the piece.

Let's Talk

My best friend and I have known each other for five years. We weren't friends at first though. We didn't even like each other for the first year and a half. But then we both started to accept each other. We learned how to put up with each other's attitudes and differing opinions. Since then we have been inseparable.

Together my friend and I learned a lesson on saying what we think to each other even if we might differ in opinion. We know that even if we disagree we will still be friends. It started in the 4th grade when I was sick. While I was sick my best friend became friends with another girl. We kept on hanging out with her so we all became really good friends.

For the rest of the year we were known as "The Three Musketeers" because we were so close. So at the end of the year we were all hoping for the same teacher at our new school. But although my best friend and I were together we weren't with the other girl. I wasn't to disappointed because I was on the same bus as her and I wanted to be with my other friend more than being with her.

Continued on next page

For a while the girl and I were always on the bus talking to each other. But then the girl got new friends. After telling my best friend about how the girl didn't really talk to me anymore my best friend admitted that she didn't really like the girl and only hanged out with the girl because I thought that she really wanted to be friends with her. And we both started to laugh.

Now we never do talk to that girl anymore. Instead we became best friends with another girl who we both liked. We still are friends with her and even closer to out new friend then with our old one. My friend and I now both express out feelings with each other because even disagreeing is better then assuming what each other thinks.

Score 1

This narrative would be more effective if it were less wordy and used more precise words. The situation is too general and lacks specific details such as names, places, and description. Words are vague and repetitive. Conventions errors include an incorrect verb form *(hanged out)*, misspellings *(to* for *too, then* for *than)*, incorrect pronouns *(I was on the same bus as <u>her</u>; <u>who</u> we both liked)*, and missing commas in compound and complex sentences.

PROMPT Write a report that gives steps, or procedures, on how to make or do something. Explain all the steps, or procedures, and materials needed.

Rubric	4	3	2	1
Focus/Ideas	How-to report well focused with clear details	How-to report generally focused with good details	How-to report often off topic; lacks clear details	How-to report with no focus or no details
Organization	Introduction and conclusion; steps in a logical order	Steps in a logical order	Steps in confused order	No attempt to put steps in order
Voice	Shows knowledge of topic; connects with audience	Pleasant voice but lacks some knowledge	Uncertain voice	No clear voice
Word Choice	Uses time-order words and strong verbs	Uses some time-order words and strong verbs	Uses few time-order words or strong verbs	No attempt to use time-order words or strong verbs
Sentences	Clear, varied sentences	Mostly clear sentences	Many unclear sentences	Incoherent sentences
Conventions	Few, if any, errors	Several minor errors	Frequent errors that detract from writing	Many serious errors that hamper understanding

How to Make a Constellation Map

Materials: pictures of constellations, tracing paper, cardboard, pen, marker, ruler, flashlight

You can map the stars in a constellation. This map will help you find the constellation among the stars in the dark night sky.

First, select one picture of a constellation. Cover the picture with tracing paper and trace the lines that connect the stars.

Next, place the tracing paper over the cardboard and punch holes in it with a pen where the stars appear (where the lines connect). Use the ruler to draw straight lines connecting the holes. Then label the cardboard with the name of the constellation. You may want to write notes on the cardboard, such as how the constellation got its name.

Finally, take the cardboard and a flashlight into a dark place, such as a closet. Hold the constellation map with the side you worked on facing down. Hold the flashlight under the map and shine the light up. You will see the constellation reflected on the ceiling.

Continued on next page

Score 4

Report focuses on one activity and explains it clearly. Writer lists materials and provides an introduction. Steps are explained clearly and succinctly, using time-order words such as *first, next, then,* and *finally*. Strong verbs *(select, trace, punch, label)* tell what to do. Sentences are fluent and concise, with varying lengths. The report shows a good understanding of writing conventions.

How to make a Chiton (KI-ton)

A chiton is what the ancient Greeks wore as clothing. A chiton looks like a toga, but instead of only having one shoulder strap, there are two. To make a chiton, you will need soft fabric or a sheet, a needle and thread or sowing machine, a tape measure, chalk, large safety pins, and a belt or rope (preferably rope).

Start by cutting two panels of fabric the length of your neck to your heel and a few inches wider than your body. Sow the panels together. Make sure that the side you don't want to be showing is the side that is showing when you sow. That way, when you turn it inside out, the seam will be on the inside, and the side of the material you like will be on the outside. When you sow, make sure you have a good, sturdy seam, or your chiton may fall apart while doing any physical activities. Then turn the chiton right side out, and make a border at the bottom (waves, boxes, squiggles, ect). Measure eighteen inches on either side and attach safety pins at both points. These will make up your shoulder straps of your chiton.

Continued on next page

> Finally, put the chiton over your head and tie a belt or rope around your waist. Put on sandals if you want to look more like a Greek. You now have completed your chiton.

Score 3

This report provides clear steps and uses precise words. The explanation of what a chiton is, and how to pronounce the word, provides context and helpful information. A list of materials is provided, and steps are presented in logical order using some time-order words. Voice is interested and pleasant, and sentences are generally clear and varied. A consistently misspelled word *(sow* for *sew)*, an incorrect abbreviation *(ect)*, as well as a couple of awkward, wordy sentences keep this from earning a top score.

How to Craft with 3-packs of Oven-Baked Clay

There are many things that you can make with 3 packs of oven-baked clay. You can almost make anything that you can think of. I will tell you how to make a dragon and a pen. After you make them you just need to use the baking instructions on the back of the package to finish them.

To make the dragon, you can use any color that you want for the body, but for this I am going to say red. Take about 1/4 of the block of red and take 1/4 of that and put it aside. Also, take two small peices of the rest to use as the arms and the hands. Take the largest section that you just seperated, and roll it up to make the serpentine body. Kind of turn that into a donut shape with one end up in the air and flatten that end. Then take the largest of the remaining peices and mold that into the shape of a dragon head that you like. Use a toothpick to help carve the mouth. Then take the head you just made and stick the head onto the flat part. After that, you can use the smaller

Continued on next page

peices to make the arms, hands, and claws. Then take a tiny bit of black and roll it into little balls to make the eyes. You can now add any more details to your dragon then bake it.

For the pen, choose 1/4 of two colors and roll both into individual balls, you will also need Bic pens that wont melt in the oven. Then flatten them until it looks like a very flat circle. Then, place one circle on top of the other and roll them up (you should see a spiral of colors), condense them into a smaller spiral, and cut off the uneven ends. Then take the ink cartridge out of the pen. Then slice off small peices from the spiral and stick them on the pen's outside making sure there are no gaps in-between. Then you are able to bake it and after that, put it back together.

There, you have a couple ideas to do with that. Now try some of your own!

Continued on next page

Score 2

This essay is really two how-to reports in one. Voice in this essay is interested and enthusiastic, but instructions are sometimes difficult to follow. There are some strong verbs and time-order words, but word choice is sometimes not specific enough to make the directions clear. There are two run-on sentences, a number of compound sentences lacking proper punctuation, and a sentence lacking agreement *(Then flatten <u>them</u> until <u>it</u> looks like a very flat circle.)*. A number of sentences begin with the word *then,* and there are several misspelled words.

Blowing Bubbles

Its easy to blow a bubble. First you must have the bubblegum and a mouth. Chew the gum for a little wile. Now push your tung against it and stick it out of you're mouth. HURRY UP and blow before it closes up but don't blow to hard or it will fly our of your mouth and you get stuff sticked all over your face! That happened to my little brother all the time.

Score 1

Pervasive errors determine this low score. Errors include many misspellings, an over-connected sentence *(HURRY…face!)*, lack of paragraph indentation, and incorrect verb forms.

Compare and contrast two people you have read about in terms of their paths to success. Choose real people or fictional characters who have achieved great things or solved problems. Tell about important similarities and differences.

Rubric	4	3	2	1
Focus/Ideas	Compare and contrast essay well focused and clearly developed	Compare and contrast essay generally focused and developed	Compare and contrast essay that strays from topic or lacks details	Compare and contrast essay with no focus or few details
Organization	Well organized; uses compare and contrast words	Organized; uses some compare and contrast words	Not clearly organized; few compare and contrast words	No organization; no compare or contrast words
Voice	Lively, engaged with topic; shows authority	Engaged with topic; shows authority	Dull; lacks authority	Not engaged with topic
Word Choice	Uses specific words to tell about similarities and differences	Uses some specific words in details	Uses few specific words in details	No attempt to use specific words
Sentences	Variety of sentences	Some variety in sentences	Little variety in sentences	Lacks sentence variety
Conventions	Few, if any, errors	Some minor errors	Errors that may confuse readers	Serious errors that obscure meaning

A Breakthrough in Science

Many women have struggled to get into the field of science and then to receive recognition for their efforts. Two famous pioneers in science, Marie Curie and Elizabeth Blackwell, faced different barriers along their roads to success. In the end, both women made an impact on future female scientists.

Marie Curie's main obstacle was financial. As a teenager, Curie worked as a teacher and governess to support her family. Later, after hard work and study, she attended the Sorbonne, a selective school in Paris. For Curie's work in chemistry and physics, she received two Nobel prizes. Through her dedication, she showed that women scientists could achieve greatness.

Elizabeth Blackwell faced a different obstacle: discrimination. Unlike Curie, Blackwell had trouble getting into school. American medical schools did not accept women. However, Blackwell persisted and was finally admitted to medical school. She eventually received her medical degree,

Continued on next page

founded an infirmary, and wrote important scientific articles. Like Curie, Blackwell inspired women to follow in her footsteps.

Both Marie Curie and Elizabeth Blackwell had to overcome obstacles to achieve their goals in science. They devoted their lives to the cause and influenced generations to come.

Score 4

Essay is focused and well elaborated. There is logical structure: The introduction identifies the two subjects being compared; the body compares the subjects; the conclusion summarizes the comparisons. Writer maintains a respectful tone toward the subjects. Specific words (*governess, chemistry, physics, infirmary*) and precise transitions (*both, unlike, however, like*) are used. Varied sentence structures make the writing pleasant to read. There is good control of conventions.

Thomas Edison and Alexander Bell

Thomas Edison and Alexander Bell are both people who achieved great things. Edison invented the light bulb in 1879 and Bell invented the telephone in 1876. Both inventions are still commonly used today.

Both inventors had rivals. Like Edison, a scientist in England named Joseph Wilson Swan was also trying to invent the light bulb at the same time as Thomas Edison. Elisha Gray and Alexander Bell were both racing to invent the telephone. Joseph Swan actually did make the first light bulb but had trouble keeping the light going at all times. Edison fixed those problems and patented his design. Elisha Gray and Bell patented their designs on the same day but Bell's design arrived at the New York patent office two hours before Elisha Gray's did.

Edison and Bell were both born into middle class families and had siblings. They also both caught serious diseases. Bell caught tuberculosis but he recovered from it. Edison had diseases with a high fever that caused him some loss of hearing.

Edison was born and raised in America. Bell was born in Scotland and than moved to Canada in his childhood.

Continued on next page

Later Bell moved to America. Another similarity between the two inventors is that even at a young age, they both loved to read and experiment with things that later helped them become inventors.

Both inventors had assistants. Bell had an assistant named Watson. Edison had a whole group of men that helped him. But the inventors did experiments in different ways. Edison worked at a different job during the day and did his experimenting at night. Bell however, spent all of his time creating the telephone. Both men were married and had kids.

Edison and Bell were two different men that shared similar interests and some similar background. They both made amazing inventions. Our lives would be very different without these two men and their important inventions we still use all the time.

Score 3

This essay addresses the prompt and uses words such as *both* and *also,* as well as similarities to compare. However, wordiness and some facts that stray a little from the topic detract from the writing. There is good control over conventions with the exception of missing commas in some compound sentences and after an introduction, and the use of *than* for *then.*

The two characters I'm compareing are Evelyn from the book Rangers Apprentice: The Icebound Land and Edie, from StoneHeart. Both girls are different from other children and face challenging problems and use their wits and their luck to get out of them.

Evelyn is a princess who was kidnapped by the Skandians, a warrior type people, who intend to keep her as a slave. She quickley learns how to survive the life of a slave, and with some help from a pitying Skandian warrior escapes and is forced to survive on her wits in the wild.

Edie is a glint, a person who can tell the past of a stone she touches. Glints can also see the moving stone figures which normal people can't see because their brains can't comprehend the possibility of statues walking around. The statues constantly attak her, so she is almost always on the run thinking about where to hide next.

Continued on next page

> Both girls live challenging lives and are incredably smart for their age and amount of experience. They live lives of challenge and adventure.

Score 2

This essay addresses the prompt and uses words such as *both* and *different,* but gives few details to describe how the two girls are specifically alike or different. Details explain each girl's situation, but stray from the main focus and do not explain how one situation compares to the other. In addition, misspellings and lack of punctuation help account for the score.

My Mom and My Grandma

My mom and my grandma are alike because they both work really hard. My mom is a kindergarden teacher and works hard everyday. She also is in graduate school and has homework every week. She is also my volleyball coach, plus she plays volleyball every Wednesday. On top of this my mom has to take care of the family by cooking and cleaning. My grandma used to work at a bank, but now she is retired. She takes care of my grandpa who is very picky He has to have everything perfect in the way he likes it. This is hard enough for my grandma, but my grandpa got hurt when he was in Europe and now has two casts on his legs. To take care of a man with two broken legs is very difficult for one person. On top of all of this chaos the family comes over to my grandma's house on Sunday. That helps her when she has to take care of Grandpa, but she also has to take care of all her grandchildren. Sometimes

Continued on next page

when life is too busy, my grandma and my mom go out to see a play or something while my sisters and I take care of our grandpa. My mom and my grandma are different because my mom works as a teacher and my grandma works as a housewife. My mom and grandma are very special to me because of their path to success. One day I want to be just like them.

Score 1

This essay does not appropriately address the prompt. The writer's subjects are not people she has read about; they are family. Only one direct comparison and one difference are specifically addressed. Many details about each subject are provided, but the writer does not explain the ways in which these details show similarities or differences. In addition, errors in conventions, particularly punctuation, detract from the writing.

Write a story about an adventure, a discovery, or something that happened to you for the first time. Use some of these literary devices: foreshadowing, tension, suspense, conflict, humor.

Rubric	4	3	2	1
Focus/Ideas	Story strongly focused on one exciting event or experience	Story generally focused on one exciting event or experience	Story often off topic; event or experience not exciting	Story with no focus
Organization	Well organized with clear beginning, middle, and end	Has a beginning, middle, and end	Unclear beginning, middle, and end	Lacks a beginning, middle, and/or end
Voice	Voice of character or narrator engaging, believable	Voice of character or narrator generally believable	Character or narrator lacking distinct voice	Voice of character or narrator not believable
Word Choice	Time-order words show sequence; vivid words create interest	Uses some time-order transition and vivid words	Uses few time-order transition or vivid words	No attempt to use time-order or vivid words
Sentences	Clear sentence, varied in types	Mostly clear sentences with some variety	Some sentences unclear; little or no variety	Incoherent or short, choppy sentences
Conventions	Few, in any, errors	Several minor errors	Many errors that detract from writing	Serious errors that hamper understanding

Trip to Planet X

Suddenly the satellite's signal disappeared from the screen. We had followed satellite GX17 since it was knocked out of its orbit by a meteoroid. The satellite carried valuable instruments and data, and we needed to find it. It couldn't have just disappeared. Jackson and I had to find out what really happened to GX17.

We flew toward where we had last seen the satellite's signal. After many hours, an orange mass came into view. It appeared to be a very small planet. Had the satellite hit the planet? We didn't know. But exploring this mysterious place was an opportunity Jackson and I couldn't pass up.

We were trembling with anticipation as we stepped out onto the planet. All around us were deep orange craters and wide valleys. The sky was a pale yellow without a single cloud. We spotted part of the satellite 100 yards away and hiked toward it.

The satellite was in pieces. Luckily, the recording equipment was unharmed, We took photos of the planet with the satellite's camera and collected a soil sample. We needed proof to take home. Our suits were running low on oxygen; it was time to head back to the ship.

Continued on next page

> On the way home, Jackson and I could not keep the smiles off our faces. Not only did we find the satellite, but we had discovered something extraordinary—an unknown planet.

Score 4

Story is focused on the quest to find the lost satellite. Paragraphs are smoothly connected. Writer uses literary elements such as foreshadowing, suspense, and conflict to make the story exciting. Specific words and vivid imagery keep the reader interested. Varied sentence lengths and structures create a rhythm that fits the action in the story. Writer has excellent control of grammar, capitalization, spelling, and punctuation.

The Mystery in the Barn

As my sister Abby and I approached the barn, chills ran up my spine. Its just the old weathered barn behind Grandma's house, I thought. But I feared what might be in it. Grandma always kept the barn doors tightly locked. What could be inside?

Grandma was making dinner, but she would be wondering where we were. We didn't want to worry her, so we had to hurry. I yanked a loose board on the side of the barn, and Abby wiggled inside. At first, Abby was silent. Then she yelled Whoa! I helped her squeeze back through the boards.

"What did you see" I asked excitedly?

"You know that car you and Dad are always talking about? The red convertible? Well, its in there under a dusty tarp." I couldnt believe it! Grandma had been keeping a sports car in her barn?

Just then we heard footsteps. Abby and I tried to run and hide, but Grandma had seen us. "Isn't it a great gift" she said? A gift for who? I wondered. It turned out that the car had been Grandpa's. It had got all grungy since he died. Grandma had it restored as a birthday surprise for

Continued on next page

> our dad. Abby and me would keep her secret. I couldn't wait
> for Dad to discover the mystery inside the barn for himself.

Score 3

This story is lively and well paced. The first paragraph develops a mood
of suspense to build up to the discovery of the car. Word choice is precise
(weathered, yanked, wiggled). A few errors prevent the story from receiving
a top score. Some contractions are misspelled, quotations are sometimes
incorrectly punctuated, and there are two pronoun errors. *(A gift for <u>who</u>?
Abby and <u>me</u> would keep her secret.)*

Treasure Hunt

Andrew and Jose wanted to find a treasure map leading to untold riches. They dug a hole and found an old glass bottle with a note inside. The note was in black cursive and had a tiny tint to it. It smelled like tea and burned paper. They opened it with fear and a shiver down their back. The note said "Look high and low side to side eventually you'll find it." They didn't know what it was. They started pitching ideas cookies, games, toys, treasure, and money! Jose said, "The old paper? It must be a clue to a treasure!" "Yes your right it must be!" said Andrew. They started looking high and low side to side. After five minutes they gave up. Jose was hanging out by the tree and saw another old glass bottle up high in the tree. Andrew came running over. Andrew said "I'll get it because I'm in gymnastics and climbing trees is good practice." He climbed where the bottle was and tossed it to Jose. Andrew came down and together they opened the bottle. It was a map!! The map was leading to a big red X. Jose said "It's a treasure map!!" "Are you sure?" Andrew asked "Yes I am sure because X marks the

Continued on next page

spot!!!" Jose said "Ok, ok, ok well what are you waiting for let's go find it!!!" Andrew said "The first place it says to go is to the super market then look for orange." Jose said. They walked over to the super market they started looking for the next clue. "The note said orange we have to look for something orange." Andrew said "Well I got that when the clue said look for orange." Jose said. "That's odd there's an orange tub in the oranges." Andrew said "That's the clue" They both said. They both opened it and it said "Bring a shovel and a pail look by the biggest tree in the park it's going to be messy." "The park lets go home to get a shovel and a pail then to the park we go." Jose said. They got a shovel and a pail then they walked to the park. "Look for the biggest tree" Andrew said. They found the biggest tree and started to dig. "I found it I found it I found it" Jose said. They brought it out to open. There was a note on the box. "A key will open no key will not." They started looking for a key. They flipped the box on its side and upside down. The key was under the box. They took the key and put it in the lock. Little by little they turned the key. "Pop" the top of the

Continued on next page

box went. They took a look inside there were cookies, games, toys, treasure, and money they were so happy. They put all the stuff back and brought it home they showed Jose's mom and his mom already knew because she started the treasure hunt.

Score 2

This is an exciting story with some vivid details. However, the writer has failed to include a few critical story details to tie all the events together. Numerous and pervasive punctuation errors, as well as a lack of paragraph indentation, also seriously detract from a reader's ability to clearly understand what is happening in the story.

Big Roller

    Last year I rode a roller coaster for the first time. It was COOL! We went really fast and really high, and the people on the ground looked small. You feel like you're a king up there. My sister rocked the cage, and that made me really nervous. But it was an awesome experience and is one that I hope to do again.

Score 1

This piece lacks the beginning-middle-end structure and development of a story. The word *really* is overused. Although the piece is free of mechanical errors, it is too sketchy to merit a higher score.

PROMPT

Write an argument/persuasive essay for your classmates about something you would like to change at school. State your position, or claim, supporting it with examples and reasons to convince the reader of your point of view.

Rubric	4	3	2	1
Focus/Ideas	Essay with clear position, or claim, and strong reasons	Essay with position, or claim, and good reasons	Essay with vague position, or claim, and few or weak reasons	Essay with no position, claim, or reasons
Organization	Position or claim at beginning; well-developed reasons in logical order	Position or claim at beginning; reasons in order	Position or claim not at beginning; reasons in no discernible order	No position, claim, or reasons in order
Voice	Serious and persuasive	Mostly serious and persuasive	Not involved enough with topic	Not involved at all with topic
Word Choice	Uses persuasive words and vivid adjectives	Uses some persuasive words and vivid adjectives	Uses few persuasive words or vivid adjectives	Uses no persuasive words or vivid adjectives
Sentences	Well-constructed, varied sentences	Good sentences; some variety	Too many short, choppy sentences; little variety	Mostly fragments and run-on sentences
Conventions	Few, if any, errors	Several minor errors	Errors that detract from writing	Serious errors that prevent understanding

Cell Phones

Imagine that you are at school. You are doing work in your classroom and you suddenly hear a phone ring. Wouldn't that distract you and make you lose concentration? I don't think cell phones should be allowed in classrooms. They distract students and teachers, and they can also be used to cheat.

Cell phones distract students and teachers. If a class is doing work and someone's phone rings, it will cause the students to stop doing their assignment. They look around the classroom and try to figure out whose phone it was. Cell phones in class can also distract teachers. If a teacher is going over a lesson in class and a student's phone rings, the teacher will have to stop teaching the lesson in order to deal with the student. This will also distract pupils because the lesson has been interrupted. When the teacher gets back to the lesson, he/she can forget where they were in the lesson, and that can throw the class off. Many people probably think that their cell phone wouldn't be distracting, but just today, a student's cell phone rang while the class was taking Social Studies notes and the whole class got distracted and started talking.

Continued on next page

Students might also use cell phones for cheating on tests. A student can text message answers from under their desk or from the bathroom. While students do this, they can get caught and get in a lot of trouble for antics such as this. Cheating is wrong, but some students will cheat if they have their cell phones.

Something I would like to change at school is allowing students bringing cell phones to class. They distract students and teachers. They can also be used to cheat. Keeping cell phones out of the classroom will make a fairer environment for all students .

Score 4

Argument is focused on the topic of allowing cell phones in classrooms. There is a logical organization, with an engaging introduction that states the writer's opinion followed by two reasons with supporting details. The essay includes a conclusion that summarizes the writer's opinion and supporting reasons. Writing is largely formal, appropriate to the form, sincere, and persuasive. Varied sentence lengths, kinds, and structures create clear and effective communication.

Computer Technology

Most of the time, schools concentrate on subjects like Math, Science, Social Studies, and English. But other skills, like computer technology and learning to type, can help students find job opportunities later on in life. A lot of schools across America have decreased the money they spend on computers and have spent it on other things. But, if schools don't begin to invest in computers, there students will have less of a chance getting a job with computers and technology.

One of the most amazing things in this world is the Internet. You can look up anything on the Internet and find out something about it. When your at school and need information about a certain topic, instead of looking for a book, you can search the Internet and find it in about ten seconds. The Internet can also help you if you forget your homework assignment. You can just go to the school website and check.

Of course, what would we be if we didn't have prescious email. Email is very helpful to a lot of people because it doesn't have to be printed out, and if schools had computers there students could work on stuff at school, and then send there work to there house to work on after school. Also,

Continued on next page

students could email there homework to there teachers so they don't waste paper.

Global warming is a big issue. When schools assign a project for kids to work on it usually involves large sheets of paper or poster boards, which is considered paper. So when a whole class of students each does a project, they use a lot of paper. But if schools got computers, they could use a program called "keynote" which let's you create a slideshow of pictures and words, so you don't have to waste paper.

So, now you know that computers are very important. The Internet, email, keynote, and other project building computer programs, help students learn skills and help save paper. With a little help, schools across America will use computers to help there students achieve greatness.

Score 3

Argument is focused on the topic of how computers in schools help students develop skills and save paper. The organization is mostly logical, with the writer's opinion stated at the beginning followed by three supporting reasons. Voice is persuasive and committed, and word choice is effective. Different types of sentences add interest and fluency. The consistent misuse of *there* for *their*, and also *your* for *you're*, as well as a misspelled word (*prescious*) and some slightly awkward sentences prevent this essay from getting a top score.

Stop the Homework Madness

We should have less homework in schools because homework kills trees and messes up your schedules. If each teacher gives you one homework assignment, then since you have a lot of classes, that's a lot of homework. So, you get home and relax for a while, then you have activities to do. Once you finish all your other activities, you have to start your homework. When you finish that you get ready for bed. In the morning at school you're very tired and you don't remember anything you did for homework. You think to yourself, please don't let the teacher give me a pop quiz because, you know if she does you will fail. Simple homework problems become big problems because you're stressed out and its very hard to think things through. Please stop the homework madness!

Continued on next page

Score 2

This essay about homework has an engaging opening, and distinct voice. However, the writer doesn't support her position with reasons or explanations. Instead, the essay seems to be about the stress of having a busy schedule. Some sentences are awkward and wordy. Numerous punctuation errors also detract from the text.

No Homework

There shouldn't be no homework on the weekends. We need time to do what we want. Like hang out with our friends and a million other things. We have too much homework during the week. We shouldn't have homework during the weekend to make time for sports and relaxing. My cousin Ray he studies maybe six hours over the weekend which I thin is ridiculous. Me and my friends prefer to just chill out.

  We should have longer recess too. Recess is too short so we should have 2 instead of 1. And pizza every day for lunch. We should have a party on Fridays and watch DVDs. We're only kids once so give us a break.

Continued on next page

Score 1

This essay is too disorganized and full of errors to be effective. The initial argument for having no weekend homework shifts to requests for longer recess, pizza for lunch, and Friday parties. Faulty conventions include a double negative *(shouldn't be no homework)*, sentence fragments, and pronoun errors *(My cousin Ray he; Me and my friends prefer to just chill out.)*.

Write a research report about an aspect of ancient culture or a civilization, such as ancient Egypt, Greece, or the Aztec empire. Make sure to write a clear thesis statement.

Rubric	4	3	2	1
Focus/Ideas	Well-focused report with strong thesis statement	Focused report with thesis statement	Report with uneven focus on thesis statement	Report lacking focus or thesis statement
Organization	Logical paragraphs with clear topic and detail sentences	Mostly logical paragraphs with topic and detail sentences	Few paragraphs with topic and detail sentences	Not in paragraphs; no topic sentences
Voice	Interested, informative voice	Generally informative voice	Weak voice; not involved enough with topic	No voice; not involved with topic
Word Choice	Evidence of paraphrasing	Some evidence of paraphrasing	Paraphrasing attempted	No paraphrasing
Sentences	Clear, varied sentences	Some sentence variety	Choppy sentences; lacks variety	Run-on sentences, fragments
Conventions	Few, if any, errors	Some minor errors	Many errors that detract from writing	Numerous errors that hinder understanding

Ancient Romans: Great Architects

Ancient Roman architecture proves that ancient Rome was an advanced civilization. Study the remains of ancient Roman buildings. The materials and unique features of the buildings show that the ancient Romans were great architects.

Ancient Roman architects used materials they found in the earth for their buildings. Some of the oldest buildings were made with rock from volcanoes called tuff. A type of limestone was used to construct the Colosseum and other buildings. Ancient Romans also used marble, bronze, stucco, and their own form of concrete.

With these materials, ancient Romans constructed beautiful buildings with unique features. Columns, used to support a building, were not only strong but elegant. The arch was another feature of Roman architecture. Arches were used for bridges and aqueducts.

Some of the most famous buildings in the world were built by the ancient Romans. The Colossuem is a huge ampitheater that could hold 45,000 people. Part of the Colosseum is still standing. Another famous building is the Pantheon, a large domed structure with columns. The inside

Continued on next page

of the Pantheon contains spectacular marble and bronze decorations.

    Ancient Roman buildings reflect the people who built them. As Encyclopedia Britannica says, "Roman architecture was almost as complex as the Roman Empire itself." The remains of the buildings they constructed show the creativity and skill of the ancient Romans.

Score 4

This report is focused on he topic of ancient Roman architecture. It is organized logically with a thesis statement followed by paragraphs with strong topic sentences and good elaboration. Writing is formal, yet engaging. Writer shows knowledge of the subject. Specific words and a supporting quotation strengthen the report. Fluent sentences have varied lengths and structures. There is excellent control of grammar, capitalization, spelling, and punctuation.

Ancient Egyptian Women

The women of ancient Egypt had an unusual degree of freedom. Even by today's standards. Thousands of years ago, other cultures were shocked that Egyptian women could pursue activities such as trading goods at the market. The rights of ordinary women, the lives of religious women, and the reigns of women pharaohs show that ancient Egyptians were ahead of their time.

Ordinary Egyptian women shared many rights with Egyptian men. Women worked at jobs besides homemaking and earned the same wages as men. Some Egyptian women even worked in the military. Women of all classes could purchase land and decide what to do with it.

A common job for women was that of priestess. Priestesses led spiritual celebrations and mourned the dead, they had a voice in politics and a position of leadership in society.

Some women even became pharaohs. Pharaohs were rulers of ancient Egypt. Six women, begining with Neithikret around 2148 B.C. and ending with Cleopatra VII in 30 B.C., reigned as pharaoh. They led the military, financial, and social activities of ancient Egypt.

Continued on next page

> Ancient Egyptian women enjoyed rights that women in other cultures have won only recently. In fact, many women are currently struggling to achieve the legal and financial equality that ancient Egyptian women had.

Score 3

This research report is organized logically with a strong thesis statement followed by paragraphs with clear topic sentences. The tone is matter-of-fact, yet personable. Writer shows knowledge of the subject. Word choice is effective, and sentences are varied. A misspelling *(begining)*, a fragment, and a run-on prevent the report from getting a top score.

Greek Mythology

Ancient Greek mythology is one of my favorite parts about the culture of ancient Greece. There are many gods and goddesses in Greek mythology. There is just so much that will catch your eye. I will tell you about some of them, but I will only be scratching the surface.

Three of the major gods and goddesses (Zeus, Poseidon, and Hades) are brothers decended from the mighty titans Cronus, king of the titans and Rhea. Zeus is most likely the most famous of the three, and the youngest. When Zeus was born, his father (Cronus) wished to swallow him as he had Zeus' other siblings including Poseidon and Hades, but his mother hid him in a cave. When he was older he caused Cronus to vomit up his brothers and sisters, who joined him in fighting the titans. Once the gods had defeated them, they imprisoned the mighty titans in the underworld of Tartarus. Afterwards the three brothers split the power of creation among themselves. Posidon received the sea as his domain Hades took the underworld, and Zeus chose the

Continued on next page

> sky. Zeus was also granted supreme authority over Mount Olympus (home of the gods) and Earth.
>
> These are only small details about the huge culture of the ancient Greek culture. There is much more to know about it.

Score 2

The information provided is interesting and specific, although there isn't a thesis statement, only an opening paragraph that establishes that the writer will discuss Greek gods and goddesses. Voice in interested and informative, but often too informal for this type of report. Word choice is vivid and specific. However, lack of punctuation as well as a few spelling errors help account for the low score.

The Mayan Calender

Of all the ancient civilizations, the mayan had the most spectacular calenders of all. The mayans had three different calenders that are paralel. They are called, Long count, Tzolkin (divine calendar), and the Haab (civil calendar). Of all these calendars, Haab has a directional relationship to the length of a year. Of the three calendars, Tzolkin is the most interesting. It is a combination of two week lengths. It contains a numberd week of 13 days from 1-13. There are 20 names in the week of 20 days in which the names are: Ahua, Imix, Ik, Akbal, Kan, Chiccan, Cimi, Manik, Lamat, Muluc, Oc, Chuen, Eb, Ben, Ix, Men, Cib, Caban, Etznab, and Caunac.

The mayans were very prescise and intelligent people. It was incredible that the mayans were able to predict so many patterns. Although, when you consider how prescise our world is, is it really a wonder we were able to compute such things?

Continued on next page

Score 1

Though the report addresses the prompt, the information the writer includes is difficult to understand or follow. The facts and information provided appear to have been transcribed or paraphrased without the writer fully understanding the meaning. In addition, numerous errors in capitalization, spelling, and punctuation seriously detract from the report.

Weekly Rubrics

Rubric	6	5	4	3	2	1
Focus/Ideas	Narrative well focused with many supporting details	Narrative mostly well focused with several supporting details	Narrative generally focused with supporting details	Narrative often off topic; lacks supporting details	Narrative with little to no focus or insufficient information	Narrative with no focus or insufficient information
Organization	Clear sequence of events with time-order words	Mostly clear sequence of events with time-order words	Reasonably clear sequence with one or two lapses	Confused sequence of events	Little attempt to put events into sequence	No attempt to put events into sequence
Voice	Sincere, engaging, and unique voice that shows rather than tells	Sincere, engaging, and unique voice that mostly shows rather than tells	Pleasant voice that occasionally shows, rather than tells	No clear, original voice; tells rather than shows	No clear or original voice; somewhat uninvolved or indifferent; tells rather than shows	Uninvolved or indifferent; poor telling; no showing
Word Choice	Vivid descriptive words that invoke a sensory response	Vivid descriptive words; generally invoke a sensory response	Some vivid words that describe subjects	Few vivid words that describe subjects	One or two vivid words that describe subjects	No attempt to use vivid, sensory words
Sentences	Clear sentences; variety of sentence types	Mostly clear sentences; good variety of sentence types	Mostly clear sentences with some variety	Some sentences unclear; little or no variety	Many sentences unclear; little or no variety	Incoherent sentences or short, choppy sentences
Conventions	Includes four kinds of sentences; few, if any, errors	Includes three or four kinds of sentences; a few minor errors	Includes three kinds of sentences; several minor errors	Includes two kinds of sentences; frequent errors that detract from writing	Includes one or two kinds of sentences; many errors that detract from writing	Includes one kind of sentence; many errors that seriously detract from writing

Rubric	5	4	3	2	1
Focus/Ideas	Personal narrative well focused with many supporting details	Personal narrative mostly well focused with several supporting details	Personal narrative generally focused with supporting details	Personal narrative often off topic; lacks supporting details	Personal narrative with no focus or insufficient information
Organization	Clear sequence of events with time-order words	Mostly clear sequence of events with strong use of time-order words	Reasonably clear sequence with one or two lapses	Confused sequence of events	No attempt to put events into sequence
Voice	Sincere, engaging, and unique voice that shows rather than tells	Sincere, engaging, and unique voice that mostly shows rather than tells	Pleasant voice that sometimes shows, rather than tells; not compelling or unique	No clear, original voice; tells rather than shows	Uninvolved or indifferent; poor telling; no showing
Word Choice	Vivid descriptive words that invoke a sensory response	Vivid descriptive words; generally invoke a sensory response	Some vivid words that describe subjects	Few vivid words that describe subjects	No attempt to use vivid, sensory words
Sentences	Clear sentences; variety of sentence types	Mostly clear sentences; good variety of sentence types	Mostly clear sentences with some variety	Some sentences unclear; little or no variety	Incoherent sentences or short, choppy sentences
Conventions	Includes four kinds of sentences; few, if any, errors	Includes three or four kinds of sentences; a few minor errors	Includes three kinds of sentences; several minor errors	Includes two kinds of sentences; frequent errors that detract from writing	Includes one kind of sentence; many errors that seriously detract from writing

Rubric	4	3	2	1
Focus/Ideas	Personal narrative well focused with many supporting details	Personal narrative generally focused with supporting details	Personal narrative often off topic; lacks supporting details	Personal narrative with no focus or insufficient information
Organization	Clear sequence of events with time-order words	Reasonably clear sequence with one or two lapses	Confused sequence of events	No attempt to put events into sequence
Voice	Sincere, engaging, and unique voice that shows rather than tells	Pleasant voice that sometimes shows, rather than tells; not compelling or unique	No clear, original voice; tells rather than shows	Uninvolved or indifferent; poor telling; no showing
Word Choice	Vivid descriptive words that invoke a sensory response	Some vivid words that describe subjects	Few vivid words that describe subjects	No attempt to use vivid, sensory words
Sentences	Clear sentences; variety of sentence types	Mostly clear sentences with some variety	Some sentences unclear; little or no variety	Incoherent sentences or short, choppy sentences
Conventions	Includes four kinds of sentences; few, if any, errors	Includes three kinds of sentences; several minor errors	Includes two kinds of sentences; frequent errors that detract from writing	Includes one kind of sentence; many errors that seriously detract from writing

Rubric	6	5	4	3	2	1
Focus/Ideas	Excellent focused narrative; well elaborated with quality details	Generally focused narrative; elaborated with telling details	Occasionally focused narrative; needs more supporting details	Sometimes unfocused narrative; needs more supporting details	Mostly unfocused narrative; lacking in development and details	Rambling narrative; lacks development and details
Organization	Organized logically; strong introduction	Organized logically; fairly strong introduction	Organized somewhat logically; introduction somewhat unclear	Organizational pattern attempted but not clear; weak introduction	Little organizational pattern; weak introduction	No organizational pattern evident; introduction weak or nonexistent
Voice	Writer closely involved; engaging personality	Sincere voice but not fully engaged	Sincere voice, but very little engagement with reader	Little writer involvement, personality	Little writer involvement; very little feeling	Careless writing with no feeling
Word Choice	Vivid, precise words that bring letter to life	Accurate word choice	Somewhat accurate word choice, but limited or repetitive	Limited or repetitive word choice	Limited and repetitive word choice; sometimes incorrect word choice	Incorrect or very limited word choice
Sentences	Excellent variety of sentences; natural rhythm	Correctly constructed sentences; some variety	Sentences correctly constructed; little variety	May have simple, awkward, or wordy sentences; little variety	Choppy sentences; a few run-ons or incomplete sentences	Choppy; many incomplete or run-on sentences
Conventions	Excellent control; subjects and predicates used correctly	Reasonable control; subjects and predicates generally used correctly	Adequate control; a few subject and predicate errors	Weak control; subjects and predicates used incorrectly	Weak control with many errors	Many errors that prevent understanding

Rubric	5	4	3	2	1
Focus/Ideas	Excellent focused narrative; well elaborated with quality details	Generally focused narrative; elaborated with telling details	Sometimes unfocused narrative; needs more supporting details	Mostly unfocused narrative; lacking in development and details	Rambling narrative; lacks development and details
Organization	Organized logically; strong introduction	Organized logically; fairly strong introduction	Organizational pattern attempted but not clear; weak introduction	Little organizational pattern; weak introduction	No organizational pattern evident; introduction weak or nonexistent
Voice	Writer closely involved; engaging personality	Sincere voice but not fully engaged	Little writer involvement, personality	Little writer involvement; very little feeling	Careless writing with no feeling
Word Choice	Vivid, precise words that bring letter to life	Accurate word choice	Limited or repetitive word choice	Limited and repetitive word choice; sometimes incorrect word choice	Incorrect or very limited word choice
Sentences	Excellent variety of sentences; natural rhythm	Correctly constructed sentences; some variety	May have simple, awkward, or wordy sentences; little variety	Choppy sentences; a few run-ons or incomplete sentences	Choppy; many incomplete or run-on sentences
Conventions	Excellent control; subjects and predicates used correctly	Reasonable control; subjects and predicates generally used correctly	Weak control; subjects and predicates used incorrectly	Weak control with many errors	Many errors that prevent understanding

Rubric	4	3	2	1
Focus/Ideas	Excellent focused narrative; well elaborated with quality details	Generally focused narrative; elaborated with telling details	Sometimes unfocused narrative; needs more supporting details	Rambling narrative; lacks development and details
Organization	Organized logically; strong introduction	Organized logically; fairly strong introduction	Organizational pattern attempted but not clear; weak introduction	No organizational pattern evident; introduction weak or nonexistent
Voice	Writer closely involved; engaging personality	Sincere voice but not fully engaged	Little writer involvement, personality	Careless writing with no feeling
Word Choice	Vivid, precise words that bring letter to life	Accurate word choice	Limited or repetitive word choice	Incorrect or very limited word choice
Sentences	Excellent variety of sentences; natural rhythm	Correctly constructed sentences; some variety	May have simple, awkward, or wordy sentences; little variety	Choppy; many incomplete or run-on sentences
Conventions	Excellent control; subjects and predicates used correctly	Reasonable control; subjects and predicates generally used correctly	Weak control; subjects and predicates used incorrectly	Many errors that prevent understanding

Rubric	6	5	4	3	2	1
Focus/Ideas	Clear, focused poem	Most ideas are clear and focused	A few clear and focused ideas	Some ideas in poem unclear	Many ideas in poem unclear	Poem lacks focus
Organization	Organized logically	Mostly well organized	Generally well organized	Unclear organization	Organization is very unclear	Poor organization
Voice	Strong voice, shows writer's feelings	Evident voice	Voice is evident but sometimes weak	Weak voice	Weak voice	No clear voice
Word Choice	Vivid, precise word choice that creates strong images; excellent use of sensory details and poetic techniques	Good word choice and imagery; good use of sensory details and poetic techniques	Adequate word choice and imagery; adequate use of sensory details and poetic techniques	Fair word choice; weak imagery; few attempts at using sensory details and poetic techniques	Limited word choice; little attempt at imagery; one or two attempts at using sensory details and poetic techniques	Limited word choice; no attempts at imagery, sensory details, or use of poetic techniques
Sentences	Meaningful within the conventions of poetry; shows rhythm	Fairly good sentences within poetic conventions; attempt at rhythm	Adequate sentences within poetic conventions; weak attempt at rhythm	Sentences and rhythm unclear	Sentences have few poetic conventions and make little attempt at rhythm	Sentences ignore poetic conventions and make no attempt at rhythm
Conventions	Accurate use of dependent and independent clauses	Good use of dependent and independent clauses	Adequate use of dependent and independent clauses	Clauses poorly constructed	Clauses poorly constructed; a few clauses contain serious errors	Serious errors in construction of clauses

Rubric	5	4	3	2	1
Focus/Ideas	Clear, focused poem	Most ideas are clear and focused	Some ideas in poem unclear	Many ideas in poem unclear	Poem lacks focus
Organization	Organized logically	Mostly well organized	Unclear organization	Organization is very unclear	Poor organization
Voice	Strong voice, shows writer's feelings	Evident voice	Weak voice	Weak or no clear voice	No clear voice
Word Choice	Vivid, precise word choice that creates strong images; excellent use of sensory details and poetic techniques	Good word choice and imagery; good use of sensory details and poetic techniques	Fair word choice; weak imagery; few attempts at using sensory details and poetic techniques	Limited word choice; little attempt at imagery; one or two attempts at using sensory details and poetic techniques	Limited word choice; no attempts at imagery, sensory details, or use of poetic techniques
Sentences	Meaningful within the conventions of poetry; shows rhythm	Fairly good sentences within poetic conventions; attempt at rhythm	Sentences and rhythm unclear	Sentences have few poetic conventions and make little attempt at rhythm	Sentences ignore poetic conventions and make no attempt at rhythm
Conventions	Accurate use of dependent and independent clauses	Good use of dependent and independent clauses	Clauses poorly constructed	Clauses poorly constructed; a few clauses contain serious errors	Serious errors in construction of clauses

Rubric	4	3	2	1
Focus/Ideas	Clear, focused poem	Most ideas are clear and focused	Some ideas in poem unclear	Poem lacks focus
Organization	Organized logically	Mostly well organized	Unclear organization	Poor organization
Voice	Strong voice, shows writer's feelings	Evident voice	Weak voice	No clear voice
Word Choice	Vivid, precise word choice that creates strong images; excellent use of sensory details and poetic techniques	Good word choice and imagery; good use of sensory details and poetic techniques	Fair word choice; weak imagery; few attempts at using sensory details and poetic techniques	Limited word choice; no attempts at imagery, sensory details, or use of poetic techniques
Sentences	Meaningful within the conventions of poetry; shows rhythm	Fairly good sentences within poetic conventions; attempt at rhythm	Sentences and rhythm unclear	Sentences ignore poetic conventions and make no attempt at rhythm
Conventions	Accurate use of dependent and independent clauses	Good use of dependent independent clauses	Clauses poorly constructed	Serious errors in construction of clauses

Rubric	6	5	4	3	2	1
Focus/Ideas	Ideas well focused; strong supporting details; clear and convincing problem and solution	Ideas focused; a few strong supporting details; clear problem and solution	Ideas somewhat focused; some supporting details; fairly clear problem and solution	Ideas have weak focus; some supporting details; problem and solution lack clarity	Weak focus; few supporting details; vague problem and solution	No focus to ideas; no supporting details; no clear problem or solution
Organization	Organized logically; strong topic sentence	Organized logically; good topic sentence	Organized logically; fairly strong topic sentence	Organization is somewhat logical; adequate topic sentence	Organization attempted but unclear; weak topic sentence	No organizational pattern evident; topic sentence weak or nonexistent
Voice	Engaging; shows writer's feelings about subject	Mostly engaging; shows writer's feelings about subject	Evident voice connecting with reader	Voice is evident but somewhat weak	Weak voice	Flat writing with no identifiable voice
Word Choice	Vivid, precise word choice	Several vivid, precise word choices	Accurate word choice	Mostly accurate but occasionally limited word choice	Limited or repetitive word choice	Incorrect or very limited word choice
Sentences	Varied sentences including compound and complex sentences	Some variation in sentences including compound and complex sentences	Not as much variety; compound and complex sentences included	Little variety; compound and complex sentences occasionally incorrect	Too many similar sentences; few or no compound or complex sentences	Many fragments and run-ons; no compound or complex sentences
Conventions	Excellent accuracy; compound and complex sentences punctuated correctly	Strong control; compound and complex sentences punctuated correctly	Good control; few errors; compound and complex sentences generally correct	Several minor errors in compound and complex sentences	Weak control; compound and/or complex sentences used incorrectly	Serious errors that obscure meaning

Rubric	5	4	3	2	1
Focus/Ideas	Ideas well focused; strong supporting details; clear and convincing problem and solution	Ideas focused; a few strong supporting details; clear problem and solution	Ideas somewhat focused; some supporting details; fairly clear problem and solution	Weak focus; few supporting details; vague problem and solution	No focus to ideas; no supporting details; no clear problem or solution
Organization	Organized logically; strong topic sentence	Organized logically; good topic sentence	Organization includes topic sentence	Organization attempted but unclear; weak topic sentence	No organizational pattern evident; topic sentence weak or nonexistent
Voice	Engaging; shows writer's feelings about subject	Mostly engaging; shows writer's feelings about subject	Evident voice connecting with reader	Weak voice	Flat writing with no identifiable voice
Word Choice	Vivid, precise word choice	Several vivid, precise word choices	Accurate word choice	Limited or repetitive word choice	Incorrect or very limited word choice
Sentences	Varied sentences including correct use of compound and complex sentences	Some variation in sentences including compound and complex sentences	Not as much variety; mostly correct use of compound and complex sentences	Many similar sentences; few compound or complex sentences	Many fragments and run-ons; no compound or complex sentences
Conventions	Excellent accuracy; compound and complex sentences punctuated correctly	Strong control; one or two errors; compound and complex sentences punctuated correctly	Good control; few errors; compound and complex sentences generally correct	Weak control; compound and/or complex sentences used incorrectly	Serious errors that obscure meaning

Rubric	4	3	2	1
Focus/Ideas	Ideas well focused; strong supporting details; clear and convincing problem and solution	Ideas somewhat focused; some supporting details; fairly clear problem and solution	Weak focus; few supporting details; vague problem and solution	No focus to ideas; no supporting details; no clear problem or solution
Organization	Organized logically; strong topic sentence	Organized logically; fairly strong topic sentence	Organization attempted but unclear; weak topic sentence	No organizational pattern evident; topic sentence weak or nonexistent
Voice	Engaging; shows writer's feelings about subject	Evident voice connecting with reader	Weak voice	Flat writing with no identifiable voice
Word Choice	Vivid, precise word choice	Accurate word choice	Limited or repetitive word choice	Incorrect or very limited word choice
Sentences	Varied sentences including correct use of compound and complex sentences	Not as much variety; order mostly logical; mostly correct use of compound and complex sentences	Too many similar sentences; few or no compound or complex sentences	Many fragments and run-ons; no compound or complex sentences
Conventions	Excellent accuracy; compound and complex sentences punctuated correctly	Good control; few errors; compound and complex sentences generally correct	Weak control; compound and/or complex sentences used incorrectly	Serious errors that obscure meaning

Rubric	6	5	4	3	2	1
Focus/Ideas	Clear, focused composition with effective supporting details	Mostly clear and focused composition; some supporting details	Somewhat clear and focused composition; a few supporting details	Composition somewhat unfocused; insufficient supporting details	Composition lacks focus; insufficient supporting details	Composition with no clarity or development
Organization	Organized logically; ideas are coherent and focused	Organized logically; few gaps; ideas fairly focused and coherent	Organized somewhat logically; many gaps; ideas somewhat focused and coherent	Organization attempted but not clear; some ideas unrelated to subject	Organization attempted, but many ideas unrelated to the subject	Poor organization; ideas lack focus
Voice	Engaging; clearly expresses writer's thoughts	Evident voice; shares some thoughts and feelings	Voice is evident but sometimes weak; shares some thoughts and feelings	Weak voice; does not share many thoughts and feelings	Very weak voice; shares only one or two thoughts and feelings	Lacking clear voice
Word Choice	Vivid, precise word choice	Accurate word choice	Occasionally accurate word choice; some limited or repetitive word choice	Limited or repetitive word choice	Very limited word choice	Inaccurate or confusing word choice
Sentences	Varied sentences	Not as much variety	Some variety, but too many similar sentences	Little sentence variety	Too many similar sentences; a few fragments and run-ons	Many fragments and run-ons
Conventions	Excellent control and accuracy; common and proper nouns used correctly	Good control; few errors; common and proper nouns generally correct	Adequate control; many minor errors; common and proper nouns often incorrect	Weak control; errors with common and proper nouns	Very weak control; a few serious errors that hamper meaning	Serious errors that obscure meaning

Rubric	5	4	3	2	1
Focus/Ideas	Clear, focused composition with effective supporting details	Mostly clear and focused composition; some supporting details	Composition somewhat unfocused; insufficient supporting details	Composition lacks focus; insufficient supporting details	Composition with no clarity or development
Organization	Organized logically; ideas are coherent and focused	Organized logically; few gaps; ideas fairly focused and coherent	Organization attempted but not clear; some ideas unrelated to subject	Organization barely attempted, almost totally unclear; many ideas unrelated to the subject	Poor organization; ideas lack focus
Voice	Engaging; clearly expresses writer's thoughts	Evident voice; shares some thoughts and feelings	Weak voice; does not share many thoughts and feelings	Very weak voice; shares only one or two thoughts and feelings	Lacking clear voice
Word Choice	Vivid, precise word choice	Accurate word choice	Limited or repetitive word choice	Limited and repetitive word choice	Very limited word choice
Sentences	Varied sentences	Not as much variety	Too many similar sentences	Too many similar sentences; a few fragments and run-ons	Many fragments and run-ons
Conventions	Excellent control and accuracy; common and proper nouns used correctly	Good control; few errors; common and proper nouns generally correct	Weak control; errors with common and proper nouns	Very weak control; a few serious errors that hamper meaning	Serious errors that obscure meaning

Rubric	4	3	2	1
Focus/Ideas	Clear, focused composition with effective supporting details	Mostly clear and focused composition; some supporting details	Composition somewhat unfocused; insufficient supporting details	Composition with no clarity or development
Organization	Organized logically; ideas are coherent and focused	Organized logically; few gaps; ideas fairly focused and coherent	Organization attempted but not clear; some ideas unrelated to subject	Poor organization; ideas lack focus
Voice	Engaging; clearly expresses writer's thoughts	Evident voice; shares some thoughts and feelings	Weak voice; does not share many thoughts and feelings	Lacking clear voice
Word Choice	Vivid, precise word choice	Accurate word choice	Limited or repetitive word choice	Very limited word choice
Sentences	Varied sentences	Not as much variety	Too many similar sentences	Many fragments and run-ons
Conventions	Excellent control and accuracy; common and proper nouns used correctly	Good control; few errors; common and proper nouns generally correct	Weak control; errors with common and proper nouns	Serious errors that obscure meaning

Rubric	6	5	4	3	2	1
Focus/Ideas	Clearly stated opinion with many supporting details	Clearly stated opinion with some supporting details	Opinion is stated with a few supporting details	Opinion is stated; some details are unclear or off topic	Opinion is stated, but few or no supporting details	Opinion is unclear with few or no supporting details
Organization	Organized logically, no gaps	Organized logically, few gaps	Organized somewhat logically, with a few gaps	Organizational pattern attempted but not clear	Organizational pattern is barely evident	No organizational pattern evident
Voice	Engaging and persuasive; strong appeal to readers' emotions	Somewhat persuasive voice; adequate appeal to readers' emotions	Persuasive voice is weak; little appeal to readers' emotions	Weak voice; persuasive tone attempted but ineffective	Weak or no identifiable voice; persuasive tone is attempted but weak	Flat writing with no identifiable voice; tone is weak or nonexistent
Word Choice	Vivid, precise word choice	Accurate word choice	Somewhat accurate word choice; some limited or repetitive word choice	Limited or repetitive word choice	Limited and repetitive word choice; sometimes incorrect word choice	Incorrect or very limited word choice
Sentences	Varied sentences in logical progression	Not as much variety; order mostly logical	Little variety; order somewhat logical	Too many similar sentences	Too many similar sentences; a few fragments and run-ons	Many fragments and run-ons
Conventions	Excellent control and accuracy; regular and irregular plural nouns used correctly	Good control; regular and irregular plural nouns generally used correctly	Adequate control; regular and irregular plural nouns usage occasionally incorrect	Weak control; regular and irregular plural nouns used incorrectly	Very weak control; a few serious errors that hamper meaning	Serious errors that obscure meaning

Rubric	5	4	3	2	1
Focus/Ideas	Clearly stated opinion with many supporting details	Clearly stated opinion with some supporting details	Opinion is stated; some details are unclear or off topic	Opinion is stated, but few or no supporting details	Opinion is unclear with few or no supporting details
Organization	Organized logically, no gaps	Organized logically, few gaps	Organizational pattern attempted but not clear	Organizational pattern is barely evident	No organizational pattern evident
Voice	Engaging and persuasive; strong appeal to readers' emotions	Somewhat persuasive voice; adequate appeal to readers' emotions	Weak voice; persuasive tone attempted but ineffective	Weak or no identifiable voice; persuasive tone is attempted but weak	Flat writing with no identifiable voice; tone is weak or nonexistent
Word Choice	Vivid, precise word choice	Accurate word choice	Limited or repetitive word choice	Limited and repetitive word choice; sometimes incorrect word choice	Incorrect or very limited word choice
Sentences	Varied sentences in logical progression	Not as much variety; order mostly logical	Many similar sentences	Too many similar sentences; a few fragments and run-ons	Many fragments and run-ons
Conventions	Excellent control and accuracy; regular and irregular plural nouns used correctly	Good control; regular and irregular plural nouns generally used correctly	Weak control; regular and irregular plural nouns used incorrectly	Very weak control; a few serious errors that hamper meaning	Serious errors that obscure meaning

Rubric	4	3	2	1
Focus/Ideas	Clearly stated opinion with many supporting details	Clearly stated opinion with some supporting details	Opinion is stated; some details are unclear or off topic	Opinion is unclear with few or no supporting details
Organization	Organized logically, no gaps	Organized logically, few gaps	Organizational pattern attempted but not clear	No organizational pattern evident
Voice	Engaging and persuasive; strong appeal to readers' emotions	Somewhat persuasive voice; adequate appeal to readers' emotions	Weak voice; persuasive tone attempted but ineffective	Flat writing with no identifiable voice; tone is weak or nonexistent
Word Choice	Vivid, precise word choice	Accurate word choice	Limited or repetitive word choice	Incorrect or very limited word choice
Sentences	Varied sentences in logical progression	Not as much variety; order mostly logical	Too many similar sentences	Many fragments and run-ons
Conventions	Excellent control and accuracy; regular and irregular plural nouns used correctly	Good control; regular and irregular plural nouns generally used correctly	Weak control; regular and irregular plural nouns used incorrectly	Serious errors that obscure meaning

Rubric	6	5	4	3	2	1
Focus/Ideas	Excellent, focused narrative; well elaborated with details and suspense	Mostly focused narrative; elaborated with details and suspense	Generally focused narrative, some supporting details and suspense	Narrative sometimes focused with few details and little suspense	Narrative rarely focused with very few details and almost no suspense	Rambling narrative; lacks details and suspense
Organization	Plot includes strong beginning, middle, and end; well-developed climax	Plot includes good beginning, middle, and end; mostly well-developed climax	Plot includes coherent beginning, middle, and end; somewhat developed climax	Plot's beginning, middle, and end are weak; poorly developed climax	Plot's beginning, middle, and end are very weak; little development in climax	Plot lacks beginning, middle, and end; no apparent climax developed
Voice	Engaging, lively; shows writer's personality	Mostly engaging and lively; shows much of writer's personality	Sincere voice connects with reader	Weak voice; little writer involvement	Weak or flat writing with little feeling	Flat writing with no feeling
Word Choice	Vivid, precise words that bring story to life	Many vivid, precise words bring story to life	Some specific word choice to bring story to life	Limited or repetitive word choice	Limited word choice; some misused words	Vague, dull, or misused words
Sentences	Varied sentence structures	Not as much variety in sentence structures	Some variety to sentence structure	Some simple, awkward, or wordy sentences	Many simple, awkward, or wordy sentences	Run-on sentences; fragments
Conventions	Excellent control and accuracy; possessive nouns used correctly	Strong control and accuracy; possessive nouns used correctly	Good control, few errors; possessive nouns generally used correctly	Weak control; possessive nouns used incorrectly	Very weak control; a few serious errors that obscure meaning	Serious errors that obscure meaning

Rubric	5	4	3	2	1
Focus/Ideas	Excellent, focused narrative; well elaborated with details and suspense	Generally focused narrative, some supporting details and suspense	Narrative sometimes focused with few details and little suspense	Narrative rarely focused with very few details and almost no suspense	Rambling narrative; lacks details and suspense
Organization	Plot includes strong beginning, middle, and end; well-developed climax	Plot includes coherent beginning, middle, and end; somewhat developed climax	Plot's beginning, middle, and end are weak; poorly developed climax	Plot's beginning, middle, and end are very weak; little development in climax	Plot lacks beginning, middle, and end; no apparent climax developed
Voice	Engaging, lively; shows writer's personality	Sincere voice connects with reader	Weak voice; little writer involvement	Weak or flat writing with little feeling	Flat writing with no feeling
Word Choice	Vivid, precise words that bring story to life	Some specific word choice to bring story to life	Limited or repetitive word choice	Limited word choice; some misused words	Vague, dull, or misused words
Sentences	Varied sentence structures	Some variety to sentence structure	Some simple, awkward, or wordy sentences	Many simple, awkward, or wordy sentences	Run-on sentences; fragments
Conventions	Excellent control and accuracy; possessive nouns used correctly	Good control, few errors; possessive nouns generally used correctly	Weak control; possessive nouns used incorrectly	Very weak control; a few serious errors that obscure meaning	Serious errors that obscure meaning

Rubric	4	3	2	1
Focus/Ideas	Excellent, focused narrative; well elaborated with details and suspense	Generally focused narrative, some supporting details some suspense	Narrative sometimes focused with few details and little suspense	Rambling narrative; lacks details and suspense
Organization	Plot includes strong beginning, middle, and end; well-developed climax	Plot includes coherent beginning, middle, and end; somewhat developed climax	Plot's beginning, middle, and end are weak; poorly developed climax	Plot lacks beginning, middle, and end; no apparent climax developed
Voice	Engaging, lively; shows writer's personality	Sincere voice connects with reader	Weak voice; little writer involvement	Flat writing with no feeling
Word Choice	Vivid, precise words that bring story to life	Some specific word choice to bring story to life	Limited or repetitive word choice	Vague, dull, or misused words
Sentences	Varied sentence structures	Some variety to sentence structure	Many simple, awkward, or wordy sentences	Run-on sentences; fragments
Conventions	Excellent control and accuracy; possessive nouns used correctly	Good control, few errors; possessive nouns generally used correctly	Weak control; possessive nouns used incorrectly	Serious errors that obscure meaning

Rubric	6	5	4	3	2	1
Focus/Ideas	Excellent, focused description; well elaborated with quality details	Mostly focused description; elaborated with several quality details	Good, focused description; elaborated with telling details	Sometimes unfocused description; needs more supporting details	Frequently unfocused description; very few supporting details	Rambling description; lacks development and detail
Organization	Compelling ideas enhanced by arrangement of and transition between lines and stanzas	Interesting ideas enhanced by good arrangement of and transition between lines	Appealing arrangement of and transitions between lines and stanzas	Little direction from beginning to end; few logical transitions between lines and stanzas	Almost no direction from beginning to end; one or two logical transitions between lines and stanzas	Lacks direction and identifiable structure; no transitions between lines and stanzas
Voice	Writer closely involved; engaging personality	Writer involved most of the time; mostly engaging personality	Reveals personality	Little writer involvement, personality	Very little writer involvement; little feeling	Careless writing with no feeling
Word Choice	Vivid, precise words that create memorable pictures	Many vivid, precise words that create strong images	Clear, interesting words to bring description to life	Somewhat limited or redundant language	Limited and redundant language	Vague, dull, or misused words
Sentences	Excellent variety of sentences; creates a natural rhythm	Strong variety of sentences; creates a frequent natural rhythm	Varied lengths, styles; generally smooth and rhythmic	May have simple, awkward, or wordy sentences; little rhythm	Choppy sentences; a few incomplete or run-on sentences; almost no rhythm	Choppy; many incomplete or run-on sentences
Conventions	Excellent control; few or no errors	Strong control; one or two minor errors	No serious errors to affect understanding	Weak control; enough errors to affect understanding	Several errors that affect understanding	Many errors that prevent understanding

Rubric	5	4	3	2	1
Focus/Ideas	Excellent, focused description; well elaborated with quality details	Good, focused description; elaborated with telling details	Sometimes unfocused description; needs more supporting details	Frequently unfocused description; very few supporting details	Rambling description; lacks development and detail
Organization	Compelling ideas enhanced by arrangement of and transition between lines and stanzas	Appealing arrangement of and transitions between lines and stanzas	Little direction from beginning to end; few logical transitions between lines and stanzas	Almost no direction from beginning to end; one or two logical transitions between lines and stanzas	Lacks direction and identifiable structure; no transitions between lines and stanzas
Voice	Writer closely involved; engaging personality	Reveals personality	Little writer involvement, personality	Very little writer involvement; little feeling	Careless writing with no feeling
Word Choice	Vivid, precise words that create memorable pictures	Clear, interesting words to bring description to life	Somewhat limited or redundant language	Limited and redundant language	Vague, dull, or misused words
Sentences	Excellent variety of sentences; creates a natural rhythm	Varied lengths, styles; generally smooth and rhythmic	May have simple, awkward, or wordy sentences; little rhythm	Choppy sentences; a few incomplete or run-on sentences; almost no rhythm	Choppy; many incomplete or run-on sentences
Conventions	Excellent control; few or no errors	No serious errors to affect understanding	Weak control; enough errors to affect understanding	Several errors that affect understanding	Many errors that prevent understanding

Rubric	4	3	2	1
Focus/Ideas	Excellent, focused description; well elaborated with quality details	Good, focused description; elaborated with telling details	Sometimes unfocused description; needs more supporting details	Rambling description; lacks development and detail
Organization	Compelling ideas enhanced by arrangement of and transition between lines and stanzas	Appealing arrangement of and transitions between lines and stanzas	Little direction from beginning to end; few logical transitions between lines and stanzas	Lacks direction and identifiable structure; no transitions between lines and stanzas
Voice	Writer closely involved; engaging personality	Reveals personality	Little writer involvement, personality	Careless writing with no feeling
Word Choice	Vivid, precise words that create memorable pictures	Clear, interesting words to bring description to life	Generally limited or redundant language	Vague, dull, or misused words
Sentences	Excellent variety of sentences; creates a natural rhythm	Varied lengths, styles; generally smooth and rhythmic	May have simple, awkward, or wordy sentences; little rhythm	Choppy; many incomplete or run-on sentences
Conventions	Excellent control; few or no errors	No serious errors to affect understanding	Weak control; enough errors to affect understanding	Many errors that prevent understanding

Rubric	6	5	4	3	2	1
Focus/Ideas	Clear, focused fantasy that addresses the prompt	Mostly clear and focused fantasy, with several supporting details	Ideas are clear and focused, but need more supporting details	Ideas are somewhat clear and focused; need several more supporting details	Writing is vague or misses the prompt	Missing fantasy genre elements or unintelligible
Organization	Strong beginning, middle, and end; well-organized paragraphs	Good beginning, middle, and end; mostly well-organized paragraphs	Recognizable beginning, middle, and end	Weak beginning, middle, and end	Plot events do not build to a climax or resolution	Plot events are random or unordered
Voice	Engaging and interesting narrator and character voices	Mostly engaging and interesting narrator and character voices	Interesting character(s) but no narrator voice	Very little drama or personality in the voice	Little drama or personality in the voice	No compelling voice
Word Choice	Vivid, precise language brings the story to life	Mostly vivid language brings the story to life	Clear details, adequate language	Somewhat clear details; language is sometimes redundant or limited	Limited or redundant language	Vague, dull, or cliché language
Sentences	Excellent variety of sentences, natural rhythm	Strong variety of sentences	Correctly constructed sentences; some variety	Sentences sometimes incorrectly constructed; little variety	Little variety; many awkward sentences	Choppy; many incomplete or run-on sentences
Conventions	Excellent control; few or no errors	Strong control; one or two minor errors	Reasonable control; few distracting errors	Weak control; several minor but distracting errors	Weak control with distracting errors	Many errors that prevent understanding

Rubric	5	4	3	2	1
Focus/Ideas	Clear, focused fantasy that addresses the prompt	Mostly clear and focused fantasy, with several supporting details	Ideas are clear and focused, but need more supporting details	Writing is vague or misses the prompt	Missing fantasy genre elements or unintelligible
Organization	Strong beginning, middle, and end; well-organized paragraphs	Good beginning, middle, and end; mostly well-organized paragraphs	Recognizable beginning, middle, and end	Plot events do not build to a climax or resolution	Plot events are random or unordered
Voice	Engaging and interesting narrator and character voices	Mostly engaging and interesting narrator and character voices	Interesting character(s) but no narrator voice	Little drama or personality in the voice	No compelling voice
Word Choice	Vivid, precise language brings the story to life	Mostly vivid language brings the story to life	Clear details, adequate language	Limited or redundant language	Vague, dull, or cliché language
Sentences	Excellent variety of sentences, natural rhythm	Strong variety of sentences	Correctly constructed sentences; some variety	Little variety; many awkward sentences	Choppy; many incomplete or run-on sentences
Conventions	Excellent control; few or no errors	Strong control; one or two minor errors	Reasonable control; few distracting errors	Weak control with distracting errors	Many errors that prevent understanding

Rubric	4	3	2	1
Focus/Ideas	Clear, focused fantasy that addresses the prompt	Ideas are clear and focused, but need more supporting details	Writing is vague or misses the prompt	Missing fantasy genre elements or unintelligible
Organization	Strong beginning, middle, and end; well-organized paragraphs	Recognizable beginning, middle, and end	Plot events do not build to a climax or resolution	Plot events are random or unordered
Voice	Engaging and interesting narrator and character voices	Interesting character(s) but no narrator voice	Little drama or personality in the voice	No compelling voice
Word Choice	Vivid, precise language brings the story to life	Clear details, adequate language	Limited or redundant language	Vague, dull, or cliché language
Sentences	Excellent variety of sentences, natural rhythm	Correctly constructed sentences; some variety	Little variety; many awkward sentences	Choppy; many incomplete or run-on sentences
Conventions	Excellent control; few or no errors	Reasonable control; few distracting errors	Weak control with distracting errors	Many errors that prevent understanding

Rubric	6	5	4	3	2	1
Focus/Ideas	Clear, focused advertisement; with relevant supporting details	Most ideas are clear and well supported	Most ideas are clear, but lack development	Sometimes focused; needs more supporting details	Most ideas are unclear and lack development	No clear ideas or development
Organization	Organized logically and displays sound reasoning throughout	Organized logically and mostly displays sound reasoning	Organization pattern somewhat unclear; some sound reasoning	Organization pattern attempted but not clear; some sound reasoning	Organizational pattern either not attempted or unclear; little sound reasoning	No clear organizational pattern; reasoning is unsound
Voice	Engaging and persuasive voice	Mostly engaging and persuasive voice	Somewhat engaging and persuasive voice	Somewhat weak voice	Weak voice, unpersuasive writing	Flat and unpersuasive writing
Word Choice	Vivid, precise word choice	Mostly precise word choice	Sometimes precise word choice, but limited or repetitive at times	Limited or repetitive word choice	Limited, often incorrect word choice	Incorrect or very limited word choice
Sentences	Varied sentences in logical progression	Good variety of sentences; order logical	Not as much variety; order logical	Too many similar sentences	Too many similar sentences; a few fragments and/or run-ons	Many fragments and run-on sentences
Conventions	Excellent control; verb tenses used correctly	Strong control; verb tenses used correctly	Good control, verb tenses generally used correctly	Sometimes weak control; verb tenses often used incorrectly	Weak control; verb tenses often used incorrectly	Many errors that seriously detract from writing

Rubric	5	4	3	2	1
Focus/Ideas	Clear, focused advertisement; with relevant supporting details	Most ideas are clear and well supported	Sometimes focused; needs more supporting details	Most ideas are unclear and lack development	No clear ideas or development
Organization	Organized logically and displays sound reasoning throughout	Organized logically and mostly displays sound reasoning	Organization pattern attempted but not clear; some sound reasoning	Organizational pattern either not attempted or unclear; little sound reasoning	No clear organizational pattern; reasoning is unsound
Voice	Engaging and persuasive voice	Mostly engaging and persuasive voice	Somewhat weak voice	Weak voice, unpersuasive writing	Flat and unpersuasive writing
Word Choice	Vivid, precise word choice	Mostly precise word choice	Sometimes limited or repetitive word choice	Limited, often incorrect word choice	Incorrect or very limited word choice
Sentences	Varied sentences in logical progression	Not as much variety; order logical	Many similar sentences	Too many similar sentences; a few fragments and/or run-ons	Many fragments and run-on sentences
Conventions	Excellent control; verb tenses used correctly	Good control; verb tenses generally used correctly	Sometimes weak control; verb tenses often used incorrectly	Weak control; verb tenses often used incorrectly	Many errors that seriously detract from writing

Rubric	4	3	2	1
Focus/Ideas	Clear, focused advertisement; with relevant supporting details	Most ideas are clear and well supported	Sometimes focused; needs more supporting details	No clear ideas or development
Organization	Organized logically and displays sound reasoning throughout	Organized logically and mostly displays sound reasoning	Organization pattern attempted but not clear; some sound reasoning	No clear organizational pattern; reasoning is unsound
Voice	Engaging and persuasive voice	Mostly engaging and persuasive voice	Weak voice	Flat and unpersuasive writing
Word Choice	Vivid, precise word choice	Mostly precise word choice	Limited or repetitive word choice	Incorrect or ver limited word choice
Sentences	Varied sentences in logical progression	Some sentence variety; order logical	Too many similar sentences	Many run-on sentences
Conventions	Excellent control; verb tenses used correctly	Good control, verb tenses generally used correctly	Weak control, verb tenses often used incorrectly	Many errors that seriously detract from writing

Rubric	6	5	4	3	2	1
Focus/Ideas	Clear, focused thesis statement addresses the prompt	Thesis is clear but may be too broad or narrow	Thesis is mostly clear, but is too broad or narrow	Thesis is vague or misses the prompt	Thesis is vague and misses the prompt	Thesis statement missing or unintelligible
Organization	Strong topic sentences and many supporting details	Most details support topic sentences	Many details support topic sentence and central thesis	Some topic sentences and some supporting details	One or two topic sentences and a few supporting details	Few details support thesis; few topic sentences
Voice	Sincere and interested	Mostly sincere and interested	Often sincere and interested; at times uninterested	Voice at times uninterested	Voice often uninterested	Writer without feeling or interest
Word Choice	Most details are unique and vivid	Many details are unique or vivid	Several details are unique or vivid	Some details are unique or vivid	Several details are vague or cliché	Most details are vague or cliché
Sentences	Uses short and long sentences of varying types	Some variety in sentence type and length	Little variety in sentence type and length	Variety only in sentence type or length	Little variety in either sentence type or length	Sentences all of one type or length
Conventions	Excellent control; few or no errors	Good control; few errors	Weak control; a few errors	Little control; many errors	Weak control; several serious errors	Many serious errors

Rubric	5	4	3	2	1
Focus/Ideas	Clear, focused thesis statement addresses the prompt	Thesis is clear but may be too broad or narrow	Thesis is mostly clear, but is too broad or narrow	Thesis is vague or misses the prompt	Thesis statement missing or unintelligible
Organization	Strong topic sentences and many supporting details	Most details support topic sentences	Many details support topic sentence and central thesis	Some topic sentences and some supporting details	Few details support thesis; few topic sentences
Voice	Sincere and interested	Mostly sincere and interested	Often sincere and interested; at times uninterested	Voice at times uninterested	Writer without feeling or interest
Word Choice	Most details are unique and vivid	Many details are unique or vivid	Several details are unique or vivid	Some details are unique or vivid	Most details are vague or cliché
Sentences	Uses short and long sentences of varying types	Some variety in sentence type and length	Little variety in sentence type and length	Variety only in sentence type or length	Sentences all of one type or length
Conventions	Excellent control; few or no errors	Good control; few errors	Weak control; a few errors	Little control; many errors	Many serious errors

Rubric	4	3	2	1
Focus/Ideas	Clear, focused thesis statement addresses the prompt	Thesis is clear but may be too broad or narrow	Thesis is vague or misses the prompt	Thesis statement missing or unintelligible
Organization	Strong topic sentences and many supporting details	Most details support topic sentences	Some topic sentences and some supporting details	Few details support thesis; few topic sentences
Voice	Sincere and interested	Mostly sincere and interested	Voice at times uninterested	Writer without feeling or interest
Word Choice	Most details are unique and vivid	Many details are unique or vivid	Some details are unique or vivid	Most details are vague or cliché
Sentences	Uses short and long sentences of varying types	Some variety in sentence type and length	Variety only in sentence type or length	Sentences all of one type or length
Conventions	Excellent control; few or no errors	Good control; few errors	Little control; many errors	Many serious errors

Rubric	6	5	4	3	2	1
Focus/Ideas	Insightful, focused biography; well supported by facts	Mostly insightful, focused biography; supported by facts	Generally focused biography; supported by some facts	Sometimes unfocused biography; needs more factual support	Frequently unfocused biography; needs much more factual support	Rambling biography; lacks facts or includes made-up information
Organization	Logical, consistent flow of ideas in sequential order	Mostly logical flow of ideas in sequential order	Some flow of ideas in sequential order	Little logic or sequence in the flow of ideas	Almost no logic or sequence in the flow of ideas	Lacks structure or logical sequence
Voice	Engaging and lively voice; suited to topic	Engaging voice with some liveliness; mostly suited to topic	Some personality revealed; voice suited to topic	Little personality evident	Almost no personality evident; sometimes flat or dull voice	Flat, dull voice not suited to topic
Word Choice	Vivid, precise words; effective use of similes and/or metaphors	Many clear words express ideas; mostly effective use of similes and/or metaphors	Clear words to express ideas; tries to use similes and/or metaphors	Routine language	Routine, sometimes vague, word choice	Vague, monotonous word choice
Sentences	Strong sentences of varied lengths and structures	Good sentences of varied lengths and structures	Simple, well-constructed sentences	Sentences unclear, missing, or repetitive	Sentences unclear; a few run-ons or incomplete sentences	Run-on or incomplete sentences; disjointed
Conventions	Excellent accuracy and control; few or no errors	Strong accuracy and control; a few minor errors	Good accuracy and control; no serious errors to affect understanding	Weak accuracy and control; hastily edited	Very weak accuracy and control; hastily edited	Poor accuracy and control; errors distracting; needs editing

Rubric	5	4	3	2	1
Focus/Ideas	Insightful, focused biography; well supported by facts	Generally focused biography; supported by some facts	Sometimes unfocused biography; needs more factual support	Frequently unfocused biography; needs much more factual support	Rambling biography; lacks facts or includes made-up information
Organization	Logical, consistent flow of ideas in sequential order	Some flow of ideas in sequential order	Little logic or sequence in the flow of ideas	Almost no logic or sequence in the flow of ideas	Lacks structure or logical sequence
Voice	Engaging and lively voice; suited to topic	Some personality revealed; voice suited to topic	Little personality evident	Almost no personality evident; sometimes flat or dull voice	Flat, dull voice not suited to topic
Word Choice	Vivid, precise words; effective use of similes and/or metaphors	Clear words to express ideas; tries to use similes and/or metaphors	Routine language	Routine, sometimes vague word choice	Vague, monotonous word choice
Sentences	Strong sentences of varied lengths and structures	Simple, well-constructed sentences	Sentences unclear, missing, or repetitive	Sentences unclear; a few run-ons or incomplete sentences	Run-on or incomplete sentences; disjointed
Conventions	Excellent accuracy and control; few or no errors	Good accuracy and control; no serious errors to affect understanding	Weak accuracy and control; hastily edited	Very weak accuracy and control; hastily edited	Poor accuracy and control; errors distracting; needs editing

Rubric	4	3	2	1
Focus/Ideas	Insightful, focused biography; well supported by facts	Generally focused biography; supported by some facts	Sometimes unfocused biography; needs more factual support	Rambling biography; lacks facts or includes made-up information
Organization	Logical, consistent flow of ideas in sequential order	Some flow of ideas in sequential order	Little logic or sequence in the flow of ideas	Lacks structure or logical sequence
Voice	Engaging and lively voice; suited to topic	Some personality revealed; voice suited to topic	Little personality evident	Flat, dull voice not suited to topic
Word Choice	Vivid, precise words; effective use of similes and/or metaphors	Clear words to express ideas; tries to use similes and/or metaphors	Routine language	Vague, monotonous word choice
Sentences	Strong sentences of varied lengths and structures	Simple, well-constructed sentences	Sentences unclear, missing, or repetitive	Run-on or incomplete sentences; disjointed
Conventions	Excellent accuracy and control; few or no errors	Good accuracy and control; no serious errors to affect understanding	Weak accuracy and control; hastily edited	Poor accuracy and control; errors distracting; needs editing

Rubric	6	5	4	3	2	1
Focus/Ideas	Excellent, focused narrative; well elaborated with dramatic details	Strongly focused narrative; elaborated with some vivid details	Generally focused narrative; elaborated with some vivid details	Sometimes unfocused narrative; needs more compelling details	Often unfocused narrative; needs many more compelling details	Rambling narrative; lacks development and detail
Organization	Organized logically in a clear sequence, with a strong beginning, middle, and end	Mostly logical organization in clear sequence; strong beginning, middle, and end	Coherent beginning, middle, and end; some events lack clear sequence	Little development from beginning to middle to end	Very little development from beginning to middle to end; sequence gets lost at times	Lacks beginning, middle, or end, and events have no logical order
Voice	Engaging and lively voice; suited to topic	Mostly engaging and lively voice; suited to topic	Some personality revealed; voice suited to topic	Little personality evident	Almost no personality evident	Flat, dull voice not suited to topic
Word Choice	Vivid, precise words; effective use of sensory details	Many vivid, precise words; mostly effective use of sensory details	Clear words to express ideas; some details tell rather than show	Routine language	Routine, sometimes vague, language	Vague, monotonous word choice
Sentences	Excellent variety of sentences; natural rhythm	Strong variety of sentences; natural rhythm	Correctly constructed sentences; some variety	May have simple, awkward, or wordy sentences; little variety	Several simple, awkward, or wordy sentences; almost no variety	Choppy; many incomplete or run-on sentences
Conventions	Excellent control; verbs, objects, and complements used correctly	Strong control; verbs, objects, and complements used correctly almost every time	No serious errors to affect understanding; sentence construction generally clear	Weak control; several verbs, objects, and complements used incorrectly	Very weak control; several errors that hamper understanding	Many errors that prevent understanding

Rubric	5	4	3	2	1
Focus/Ideas	Excellent, focused narrative; well elaborated with dramatic details	Generally focused narrative; elaborated with some vivid details	Sometimes unfocused narrative; needs more compelling details	Often unfocused narrative; needs many more compelling details	Rambling narrative; lacks development and detail
Organization	Organized logically in a clear sequence, with a strong beginning, middle, and end	Coherent beginning, middle, and end; some events lack clear sequence	Little development from beginning to middle to end	Very little development from beginning to end; sequence gets lost at times	Lacks beginning, middle, or end, and events have no logical order
Voice	Engaging and lively voice; suited to topic	Some personality revealed; voice suited to topic	Little personality evident	Almost no personality evident	Flat, dull voice not suited to topic
Word Choice	Vivid, precise words; effective use of sensory details	Clear words to express ideas; some details tell rather than show	Routine language	Routine, sometimes vague, language	Vague, monotonous word choice
Sentences	Excellent variety of sentences; natural rhythm	Correctly constructed sentences; some variety	May have simple, awkward, or wordy sentences; little variety	Several simple, awkward, or wordy sentences; almost no variety	Choppy; many incomplete or run-on sentences
Conventions	Excellent control; verbs, objects, and complements used correctly	No serious errors to affect understanding; sentence construction generally clear	Weak control; several verbs, objects, and complements used incorrectly	Very weak control; several errors that hamper understanding	Many errors that prevent understanding

Rubric	4	3	2	1
Focus/Ideas	Excellent, focused narrative; well elaborated with dramatic details	Generally focused narrative; elaborated with some vivid details	Sometimes unfocused narrative; needs more compelling details	Rambling narrative; lacks development and detail
Organization	Organized logically in a clear sequence, with a strong beginning, middle, and end	Coherent beginning, middle, and end; some events lack clear sequence	Little development from beginning to middle to end; sequence gets lost	Lacks beginning, middle, or end, and events have no logical order
Voice	Engaging and lively voice; suited to topic	Some personality revealed; voice suited to topic	Little personality evident	Flat, dull voice not suited to topic
Word Choice	Vivid, precise words; effective use of sensory details	Clear words to express ideas; some details tell rather than show	Routine language	Vague, monotonous word choice
Sentences	Excellent variety of sentences; natural rhythm	Correctly constructed sentences; some variety	May have simple, awkward, or wordy sentences; little variety	Choppy; many incomplete or run-on sentences
Conventions	Excellent control; verbs, objects, and complements used correctly	No serious errors to affect understanding; sentence construction generally clear	Weak control; several verbs, objects, and complements used incorrectly	Many errors that prevent understanding

FOLK TALE

Rubric	6	5	4	3	2	1
Focus/Ideas	Excellent, focused narrative; well elaborated with quality details	Mostly focused narrative; elaborated with quality details	Generally focused narrative; elaborated with telling details	Sometimes unfocused narrative; needs more supporting details	Frequently unfocused narrative; needs many more supporting details	Rambling narrative; lacks development and detail
Organization	Organized logically; strong beginning, middle, and end	Organization is mostly logical; good beginning, middle, and end	Organized logically; coherent beginning, middle, and end	Little direction from beginning to end; few order words	Almost no direction from beginning to end	Lacks beginning, middle, end; incorrect or no order words
Voice	Writer closely involved; engaging personality	Writer is involved; mostly engaging	Sincere voice but not fully engaged	Little writer involvement, personality	Almost no writer involvement, personality	Careless writing with no feeling
Word Choice	Vivid precise words that bring folk tale to life	Some vivid precise words that bring folk tale to life	Clear words to bring story to life	Somewhat limited or repetitive word choice	Limited and repetitive word choice	Incorrect or very limited word choice
Sentences	Excellent variety of sentences; natural rhythm	Good variety of sentences; natural rhythm	Correctly constructed sentences; some variety	May have simple, awkward, or wordy sentences; little variety	Simple, awkward, and/or wordy sentences; very little variety	Choppy; many incomplete or run-on sentences
Conventions	Excellent control; troublesome verbs used correctly	Strong control; troublesome verbs used correctly most of the time	No serious errors to affect understanding; troublesome verbs generally used correctly	Weak control; troublesome verbs used incorrectly	Very weak control; many errors that hamper understanding	Many errors that prevent understanding

Rubric	5	4	3	2	1
Focus/Ideas	Excellent, focused narrative; well elaborated with quality details	Generally focused narrative; elaborated with telling details	Sometimes unfocused narrative; needs more supporting details	Frequently unfocused narrative; needs many more supporting details	Rambling narrative; lacks development and detail
Organization	Organized logically; strong beginning, middle, and end	Organized logically; coherent beginning, middle, and end	Little direction from beginning to end; few order words	Almost no direction from beginning to end	Lacks beginning, middle, end; incorrect or no order words
Voice	Writer closely involved; engaging personality	Sincere voice but not fully engaged	Little writer involvement, personality	Almost no writer involvement, personality	Careless writing with no feeling
Word Choice	Vivid precise words that bring folk tale to life	Clear words to bring story to life	Generally limited or repetitive word choice	Limited or repetitive word choice	Incorrect or very limited word choice
Sentences	Excellent variety of sentences; natural rhythm	Correctly constructed sentences; some variety	May have simple, awkward, or wordy sentences; little variety	Simple, awkward, and/or wordy sentences; very little variety	Choppy; many incomplete or run-on sentences
Conventions	Excellent control; troublesome verbs used correctly	No serious errors to affect understanding; troublesome verbs generally used correctly	Weak control; troublesome verbs used incorrectly	Very weak control; many errors that hamper understanding	Many errors that prevent understanding

Rubric	4	3	2	1
Focus/Ideas	Excellent, focused narrative; well elaborated with quality details	Generally focused narrative; elaborated with telling details	Sometimes unfocused narrative; needs more supporting details	Rambling narrative; lacks development and detail
Organization	Organized logically; strong beginning, middle, and end	Organized logically; coherent beginning, middle, and end	Little direction from beginning to end; few order words	Lacks beginning, middle, end; incorrect or no order words
Voice	Writer closely involved; engaging personality	Sincere voice but not fully engaged	Little writer involvement, personality	Careless writing with no feeling
Word Choice	Vivid precise words that bring folk tale to life	Clear words to bring story to life	Generally limited or repetitive word choice	Incorrect or very limited word choice
Sentences	Excellent variety of sentences; natural rhythm	Correctly constructed sentences; some variety	May have simple, awkward, or wordy sentences; little variety	Choppy; many incomplete or run-on sentences
Conventions	Excellent control; troublesome verbs used correctly	No serious errors to affect understanding; troublesome verbs generally used correctly	Weak control; troublesome verbs used incorrectly	Many errors that prevent understanding

Rubric	6	5	4	3	2	1
Focus/Ideas	Personal narrative well focused with many supporting details	Personal narrative mostly well focused with supporting details	Personal narrative generally focused with supporting details	Personal narrative sometimes unfocused; needs a few more supporting details	Personal narrative often off topic; lacks supporting detail	Personal narrative with no focus or insufficient information
Organization	Clear sequence of events with time-order words	Mostly clear sequence of events with time-order words	Reasonably clear sequence of events with only one or two lapses	Somewhat unclear sequence of events with a few lapses	Confused sequence of events	No attempt to put events into sequence
Voice	Sincere, engaging, and unique voice	Mostly sincere, engaging, and unique voice	Pleasant voice, but not compelling or unique	Somewhat unclear voice; occasionally pleasant	No clear, original voice	Uninvolved or indifferent
Word Choice	Vivid descriptive adjectives that involve a sensory response	Many vivid descriptive adjectives that involved a sensory response	Some vivid adjectives that describe subjects	A few vivid adjectives that describe subjects	Few vivid adjectives that describe subjects	No attempt to use vivid, sensory adjectives
Sentences	Clear sentences; variety of sentence types	Clear sentences; not as much variety of types	Mostly clear sentences with some sentence variety	A few unclear sentences with little variety	Some sentences unclear; little or no variety	Incoherent sentences or short, choppy sentences
Conventions	Few, if any, errors; prepositions used correctly	A few minor errors; prepositions used correctly almost every time	Several minor errors; use of prepositions generally correct	A few serious errors; use of prepositions often incorrect	Frequent errors that detract from writing; confusing prepositions	Many errors that seriously detract from writing

Rubric	5	4	3	2	1
Focus/Ideas	Personal narrative well focused with many supporting details	Personal narrative generally focused with supporting details	Personal narrative sometimes unfocused; needs a few more supporting details	Personal narrative often off topic; lacks supporting detail	Personal narrative with no focus or insufficient information
Organization	Clear sequence of events with time-order words	Reasonably clear sequence of events with only one or two lapses	Somewhat unclear sequence of events with a few lapses	Confused sequence of events	No attempt to put events into sequence
Voice	Sincere, engaging, and unique voice	Pleasant voice, but not compelling or unique	Somewhat unclear voice; occasionally pleasant	No clear, original voice	Uninvolved or indifferent
Word Choice	Vivid descriptive adjectives that involve a sensory response	Many vivid adjectives that describe subjects	Some vivid adjectives that describe subjects	Few vivid adjectives that describe subjects	No attempt to use vivid, sensory adjectives
Sentences	Clear sentences; variety of sentence types	Mostly clear sentences with some sentence variety	A few unclear sentences with little variety	Some sentences unclear; little or no variety	Incoherent sentences or short, choppy sentences
Conventions	Few, if any, errors; prepositions used correctly	Several minor errors; use of prepositions generally correct	A few serious errors; use of prepositions often incorrect	Frequent errors that detract from writing; confusing prepositions	Many errors that seriously detract from writing

Rubric	4	3	2	1
Focus/Ideas	Personal narrative well focused with many supporting details	Personal narrative generally focused with supporting details	Personal narrative often off topic; lacks supporting detail	Personal narrative with no focus or insufficient information
Organization	Clear sequence of events with time-order words	Reasonably clear sequence of events with only one or two lapses	Confused sequence of events	No attempt to put events into sequence
Voice	Sincere, engaging, and unique voice	Pleasant voice, but not compelling or unique	No clear, original voice	Uninvolved or indifferent
Word Choice	Vivid descriptive adjectives that involve a sensory response	Some vivid adjectives that describe subjects	Few vivid adjectives that describe subjects	No attempt to use vivid, sensory adjectives
Sentences	Clear sentences; variety of sentence types	Mostly clear sentences with some sentence variety	Some sentences unclear; little or no variety	Incoherent sentences or short, choppy sentences
Conventions	Few, if any, errors; prepositions used correctly	Several minor errors; use of prepositions generally correct	Frequent errors that detract from writing; confusing prepositions	Many errors that seriously detract from writing

Rubric	6	5	4	3	2	1
Focus/Ideas	Clear and focused poem with appealing details; sequence of narrative clear	Narrative in poem somewhat focused with fairly clear sequence	Narrative in poem focused at times; sequence generally clear	Limited narrative with unclear sequence	Narrative lacks clear focus and sequence	No focus to narrative
Organization	Verses organized logically to tell story	Verses organized somewhat logically	Verses somewhat organized	Poem organized into verses	Organization attempted but unclear	No organizational pattern evident
Voice	Clear and engaging; shows writer's feelings with excellent use of figurative language	Evident voice connecting with reader; several good examples of figurative language	Fair voice connects with reader; some examples of figurative language	Weak voice that shows little connection to reader; attempts at figurative language don't work well	Voice shows no connection to reader; little attempt at figurative language	Flat writing with no identifiable voice and no discernible attempts at figurative language
Word Choice	Words create strong images; excellent use of rhyme	Good imagery and use of rhyme	Limited imagery; some attempts at rhyme	Weak imagery; few attempts at rhyme	Some evidence of imagery or rhyme	No apparent attempts at imagery or rhyme
Sentences	Meaningful within conventions of poetry; shows rhythm	Fairly good sentences within poetic conventions; attempt at rhythm	Sentences and rhythm generally clear	Sentences and rhythm unclear	Little attempt at poetic conventions or rhythm	Sentences ignore poetic conventions and make no attempts at rhythm
Conventions	Excellent accuracy and control; all personal pronouns used correctly	Good control; few errors; use of personal pronouns generally correct	Fair control; some errors; some personal pronouns used correctly	Limited control; several personal pronouns used incorrectly	Weak control; many serious errors hamper understanding; most personal pronouns used incorrectly	Serious errors that obscure meaning; personal pronouns used incorrectly

Rubric	5	4	3	2	1
Focus/Ideas	Clear and focused poem with appealing details; sequence of narrative clear	Narrative in poem somewhat focused with fairly clear sequence	Narrative in poem focused at times; sequence generally clear	Weak narrative with unclear sequence	No focus to narrative
Organization	Verses organized logically to tell story	Verses organized somewhat logically	Verses somewhat organized	Organization attempted but unclear	No organizational pattern evident
Voice	Clear and engaging; shows writer's feelings with excellent use of figurative language	Evident voice connecting with reader; several good examples of figurative language	Fair voice connects with reader; some examples of figurative language	Weak voice that shows little connection to reader; attempts at figurative language don't work well	Flat writing with no identifiable voice and no discernible attempts at figurative language
Word Choice	Words create strong images; excellent use of rhyme	Good imagery and use of rhyme	Limited imagery; some attempts at rhyme	Weak imagery; few attempts at rhyme	No apparent attempts at imagery or rhyme
Sentences	Meaningful within conventions of poetry; shows rhythm	Fairly good sentences within poetic conventions; attempt at rhythm	Sentences and rhythm generally clear	Sentences and rhythm unclear	Sentences ignore poetic conventions and make no attempts at rhythm
Conventions	Excellent accuracy and control; all personal pronouns used correctly	Good control; few errors; use of personal pronouns generally correct	Fair control; some errors; some personal pronouns used correctly	Weak control; several personal pronouns used incorrectly	Serious errors that obscure meaning; personal pronouns used incorrectly

Rubric	4	3	2	1
Focus/Ideas	Clear and focused poem with appealing details; sequence of narrative clear	Narrative in poem somewhat focused with fairly clear sequence	Weak narrative with unclear sequence	No focus to narrative
Organization	Verses organized logically to tell story	Verses organized somewhat logically	Organization attempted but unclear	No organizational pattern evident
Voice	Clear and engaging; shows writer's feelings with excellent use of figurative language	Evident voice connecting with reader; several good examples of figurative language	Weak voice that shows little connection to reader; attempts at figurative language don't work well	Flat writing with no identifiable voice and no discernible attempts at figurative language
Word Choice	Words create strong images; excellent use of rhyme	Good imagery and use of rhyme	Weak imagery; few attempts at rhyme	No apparent attempts at imagery or rhyme
Sentences	Meaningful within conventions of poetry; shows rhythm	Fairly good sentences within poetic conventions; attempt at rhythm	Sentences and rhythm unclear	Sentences ignore poetic conventions and make no attempts at rhythm
Conventions	Excellent accuracy and control; all personal pronouns used correctly	Good control; few errors; use of personal pronouns generally correct	Weak control; several personal pronouns used incorrectly	Serious errors that obscure meaning; personal pronouns used incorrectly

Rubric	6	5	4	3	2	1
Focus/Ideas	Focus on a single conflict; shows great sense of imagination	Focus mainly on single conflict; shows imagination	Unclear focus on single conflict; shows some imagination	Somewhat scattered focus; shows limited imagination	No clear focus; shows weak imagination	Rambling narrative; lacks imagination
Organization	Strong beginning, middle, end; appropriate order words	Coherent beginning, middle, end; many order words	Clear beginning, middle, end; many order words	Recognizable beginning, middle, end; some order words	Unclear or missing beginning, middle, end; few order words	Lacks beginning, middle, end; no order words
Voice	Engaging and unique voice	Pleasant voice but not compelling or unique	Voice is evident at times	No clear, original voice	Little evidence of writer's involvement	Uninvolved or indifferent
Word Choice	Vivid; creates humor or tension	Some vivid details that convey mood or description	Details used to create emotional connection	Few vivid words; little emotional connection	Some attempt to use vivid or descriptive words	No attempt to use vivid words
Sentences	Clear sentences; variety of sentences	Mostly clear sentences with good variety	Many clear sentences with some variety	Some sentences unclear; little variety	Most sentences unclear or incoherent; no variety	Incoherent sentences, or short, choppy sentences
Conventions	Few errors; pronouns and antecedents agree	Several minor errors; some pronoun-antecedent errors	Some errors; some clarity in pronoun usage	Several errors; little clarity in use of pronouns	Frequent serious errors that hamper understanding	Many serious errors that distract from writing

Rubric	5	4	3	2	1
Focus/Ideas	Focus on a single conflict; shows great sense of imagination	Focus mainly on single conflict; shows imagination	Unclear focus on single conflict; shows some imagination	Somewhat scattered focus; shows limited imagination	Rambling narrative; lacks imagination
Organization	Strong beginning, middle, end; appropriate order words	Coherent beginning, middle, end; many order words	Clear beginning, middle, end; some order words	Recognizable beginning, middle, end; few order words	Lacks beginning, middle, end; no order words
Voice	Engaging and unique voice	Pleasant voice but not compelling or unique	Voice is evident at times	No clear, original voice	Uninvolved or indifferent
Word Choice	Vivid; creates humor or tension	Some vivid details that convey mood or description	Details used to create emotional connection	Few vivid words; little emotional connection	No attempt to use vivid words
Sentences	Clear sentences; variety of sentences	Mostly clear sentences with good variety	Many clear sentences with some variety	Some sentences unclear; little or no variety	Incoherent sentences, or short, choppy sentences
Conventions	Few errors; pronouns and antecedents agree	Several minor errors; some pronoun-antecedent errors	Many serious errors; some clarity in pronoun usage	Frequent errors; little clarity in use of pronouns	Many serious errors that distract from writing

Rubric	4	3	2	1
Focus/Ideas	Focus on a single conflict; shows great sense of imagination	Focus mainly on single conflict; shows imagination	Somewhat scattered focus; shows limited imagination	Rambling narrative; lacks imagination
Organization	Strong beginning, middle, end; appropriate order words	Coherent beginning, middle, end; some order words	Recognizable beginning, middle, end; few order words	Lacks beginning, middle, end; no order words
Voice	Engaging and unique voice	Pleasant voice but not compelling or unique	No clear, original voice	Uninvolved or indifferent
Word Choice	Vivid; creates humor or tension	Some vivid details that convey mood or description	Few vivid words; little emotional connection	No attempt to use vivid words
Sentences	Clear sentences; variety of sentences	Mostly clear sentences with some variety	Some sentences unclear; little or no variety	Incoherent sentences, or short, choppy sentences
Conventions	Few errors; pronouns and antecedents agree	Several minor errors; some pronoun-antecedent errors	Frequent errors; little clarity in use of pronouns	Many serious errors that distract from writing

Rubric	6	5	4	3	2	1
Focus/Ideas	Good, focused description; well elaborated with quality details	Generally focused description; elaborated with telling details	Description focused at times; some supporting details	Sometimes unfocused description; needs more supporting details	Generally unclear description; few supporting details	Rambling description; lacks development and details
Organization	Logical order clarifies ideas; effective transition	Generally logical order; some transitions	Some logical order from beginning to end; transitions occasionally used	Organizational pattern attempted; some transitions	Little direction from beginning to end; few if any transitions	No organizational pattern evident; no transitions
Voice	Writer closely involved; engaging personality	Reveals personality	Some evidence of writer's personality	Little writer involvement, personality	Writer's personality not evident	Careless writing with no feeling
Word Choice	Vivid, precise words; effective use of sensory words	Some precise words; some use of sensory words	Fair use of precise or sensory words	Limited or repetitive word choice; no sensory words	Weak word choice	Vague, dull, or misused words
Sentences	Varied sentence structures; natural rhythm	Correctly constructed sentences, some variety	Many correctly constructed sentences	Some awkward sentences; little variety	May have simple, awkward, or wordy sentences; no variety	Choppy; many incomplete or run-on sentences
Conventions	Excellent control and accuracy; possessive pronouns used correctly	Good control, few errors; possessive pronouns generally used correctly	Fair control; possessive pronouns generally used correctly	Limited control; many possessive pronouns used incorrectly	Weak control; possessive pronouns used incorrectly	Serious errors that prevent understanding

Rubric	5	4	3	2	1
Focus/Ideas	Good, focused description; well elaborated with quality details	Generally focused description; elaborated with telling details	Description focused at times; some supporting details	Sometimes unfocused description; needs more supporting details	Rambling description; lacks development and details
Organization	Logical order clarifies ideas; effective transition	Generally logical order; some transitions	Some logical order from beginning to end; transitions occasionally used	Little direction from beginning to end; few transitions	No organizational pattern evident; no transitions
Voice	Writer closely involved; engaging personality	Reveals personality	Some evidence of writer's personality	Little writer involvement, personality	Careless writing with no feeling
Word Choice	Vivid, precise words; effective use of sensory words	Some precise words; some use of sensory words	Fair use of precise or sensory words	Limited or repetitive word choice; no sensory words	Vague, dull, or misused words
Sentences	Varied sentence structures; natural rhythm	Correctly constructed sentences, some variety	Many correctly constructed sentences	May have simple, awkward, or wordy sentences; little variety	Choppy; many incomplete or run-on sentences
Conventions	Excellent control and accuracy; possessive pronouns used correctly	Good control, few errors; possessive pronouns generally used correctly	Fair control; possessive pronouns generally used correctly	Weak control; possessive pronouns used incorrectly	Serious errors that prevent understanding

Rubric	4	3	2	1
Focus/Ideas	Good, focused description; well elaborated with quality details	Generally focused description; elaborated with telling details	Sometimes unfocused description; needs more supporting details	Rambling description; lacks development and details
Organization	Logical order clarifies ideas; effective transition	Generally logical order; some transitions	Little direction from beginning to end; few transitions	No organizational pattern evident; no transitions
Voice	Writer closely involved; engaging personality	Reveals personality	Little writer involvement, personality	Careless writing with no feeling
Word Choice	Vivid, precise words; effective use of sensory words	Some precise words; some use of sensory words	Limited or repetitive word choice; no sensory words	Vague, dull, or misused words
Sentences	Varied sentence structures; natural rhythm	Correctly constructed sentences, some variety	May have simple, awkward, or wordy sentences; little variety	Choppy; many incomplete or run-on sentences
Conventions	Excellent control and accuracy; possessive pronouns used correctly	Good control, few errors; possessive pronouns generally used correctly	Weak control; possessive pronouns used incorrectly	Serious errors that prevent understanding

74 Rubrics

Rubric	6	5	4	3	2	1
Focus/Ideas	Excellent, focused drama; well elaborated with quality details	Generally focused drama; elaborated with telling details	Fairly clear drama; some supporting details	Sometimes unfocused drama; needs more supporting details	Generally unfocused drama; few, if any, supporting details	Rambling drama; lacks development and detail
Organization	Events told in sequence; uses stage directions	Events in logical order, some stage directions	Most events in logical order; some stage directions	Events lack clear sequence; few stage directions	No coherent sequence of events; minimal stage direction	Lacking sequence of events; no stage directions
Voice	Engaging; reflects personality of the writer	Reveals personality of the writer	Writer is generally involved	Some evidence of writer involvement	Little evidence of writer's involvement	Flat writing with no identifiable voice
Word Choice	Vivid, precise word choice that brings the story to life	Accurate word choice that beings the story to life	Fair word choice; includes some words that bring story to life	Limited or repetitive word choice	Weak word choice	Incorrect or very limited word choice
Sentences	Excellent variety of sentences that reflect natural rhythm of dialogue	Varied lengths and styles that generally reflect natural rhythm of dialogue	Some sentences reflect natural rhythm of dialogue	Sentences occasionally reflect natural rhythm of dialogue	Repetitive sentences rarely reflect natural rhythm of dialogue	Choppy, incomplete sentences that don't reflect natural rhythm of dialogue
Conventions	Excellent control and accuracy; indefinite and reflexive pronouns used correctly	Good control, few errors; indefinite and reflexive pronouns generally used correctly	Fair control, some errors; indefinite and reflexive pronouns used correctly at times	Weak control, multiple errors; indefinite and reflexive pronouns used incorrectly	Several serious errors hamper understanding	Frequent serious errors that obscure meaning

Rubric	5	4	3	2	1
Focus/Ideas	Excellent, focused drama; well elaborated with quality details	Generally focused drama; elaborated with telling details	Fairly clear drama; some supporting details	Sometimes unfocused drama; needs more supporting details	Rambling drama; lacks development and detail
Organization	Events told in sequence; uses stage directions	Events in logical order, some stage directions	Most events in logical order; some stage directions	Events lack coherent sequence; few stage directions	Lacking sequence of events; no stage directions
Voice	Engaging; reflects personality of the writer	Reveals personality of the writer	Some evidence of writer's involvement	Little writer involvement	Flat writing with no identifiable voice
Word Choice	Vivid, precise word choice that brings the story to life	Accurate word choice that beings the story to life	Fair word choice; includes some words that bring story to life	Limited or repetitive word choice	Incorrect or very limited word choice
Sentences	Excellent variety of sentences that reflect natural rhythm of dialogue	Varied lengths and styles that generally reflect natural rhythm of dialogue	Some sentences reflect natural rhythm of dialogue	Repetitive sentences that rarely reflect natural rhythm of dialogue	Choppy, incomplete sentences that don't reflect natural rhythm of dialogue
Conventions	Excellent control and accuracy; indefinite and reflexive pronouns used correctly	Good control, few errors; indefinite and reflexive pronouns generally used correctly	Fair control, some errors; indefinite and reflexive pronouns used correctly at times	Weak control, multiple errors; indefinite and reflexive pronouns used incorrectly	Serious errors that obscure meaning

Rubric	4	3	2	1
Focus/Ideas	Excellent, focused drama; well elaborated with quality details	Generally focused drama; elaborated with telling details	Sometimes unfocused drama; needs more supporting details	Rambling drama; lacks development and detail
Organization	Events told in sequence; uses stage directions	Events in logical order, some stage directions	Events lack coherent sequence; few stage directions	Lacking sequence of events; no stage directions
Voice	Engaging; reflects personality of the writer	Reveals personality of the writer	Little writer involvement	Flat writing with no identifiable voice
Word Choice	Vivid, precise word choice that brings the story to life	Accurate word choice that beings the story to life	Limited or repetitive word choice	Incorrect or very limited word choice
Sentences	Excellent variety of sentences that reflect natural rhythm of dialogue	Varied lengths and styles that generally reflect natural rhythm of dialogue	Repetitive sentences that rarely reflect natural rhythm of dialogue	Choppy, incomplete sentences that don't reflect natural rhythm of dialogue
Conventions	Excellent control and accuracy; indefinite and reflexive pronouns used correctly	Good control, few errors; indefinite and reflexive pronouns generally used correctly	Weak control, multiple errors; indefinite and reflexive pronouns used incorrectly	Serious errors that obscure meaning

Rubric	6	5	4	3	2	1
Focus/Ideas	Clear and focused on important ideas; leaves out unimportant details	Generally clear and focused on important ideas; mostly leaves out unimportant details	Fairly clear focus on important ideas; occasionally includes unimportant details	Unclear focus on important ideas; includes unimportant details	Weak focus on important ideas; includes many unimportant details	Lack of focus
Organization	Logical, consistent flow of ideas; good transitions	Logical sequencing of ideas; good use of transitions	Some logical sequencing of ideas; uses transitions	Limited direction and sequence of ideas; some transitions	No clear direction or sequence of ideas; few transitions	Lacks structure and transitions
Voice	Engaging, lively; shows writer's personality	Sincere voice connects with reader	Some writer involvement	Weak voice; little writer involvement	No evidence of writer's feelings or involvement	Flat writing with no feeling
Word Choice	Vivid, precise words that bring story to life	Some specific word choice to bring story to life	Fair word choice; limited use of specific words	Limited or repetitive word choice	Poor, weak word choice	Vague, dull, or misused words
Sentences	Varied sentence structures	Good variety of sentence structures	Some variety of sentence structures	Some simple or awkward sentences; little variety	Many simple, awkward, or wordy sentences	Run-on sentences, fragments
Conventions	Excellent control and accuracy; *who* and *whom* are used correctly	Good control; few errors; *who* and *whom* generally used correctly	Fair control; *who* and *whom* occasionally used incorrectly	Limited control; *who* and *whom* used incorrectly	Weak control; many errors hamper understanding	Serious errors that obscure meaning

Rubric	5	4	3	2	1
Focus/Ideas	Clear and focused on important ideas; leaves out unimportant details	Generally clear and focused on important ideas; mostly leaves out unimportant details	Fairly clear focus on important ideas; occasionally includes unimportant details	Weak focus on important ideas; includes unimportant details	Lack of focus
Organization	Logical, consistent flow of ideas; good transitions	Logical sequencing of ideas; good use of transitions	Some logical sequencing of ideas; uses transitions	Weak direction and sequenced ideas; some transitions	Lacks structure and transitions
Voice	Engaging, lively; shows writer's personality	Sincere voice connects with reader	Some writer involvement	Weak voice; little writer involvement	Flat writing with no feeling
Word Choice	Vivid, precise words that bring story to life	Some specific word choice to bring story to life	Fair word choice; limited use of specific words	Limited or repetitive word choice	Vague, dull, or misused words
Sentences	Varied sentence structures	Good variety of sentence structures	Some variety of sentence structures	Many simple, awkward, or wordy sentences	Run-on sentences, fragments
Conventions	Excellent control and accuracy; *who* and *whom* are used correctly	Good control; few errors; *who* and *whom* generally used correctly	Fair control; *who* and *whom* occasionally used incorrectly	Weak control; *who* and *whom* used incorrectly	Serious errors that obscure meaning

Rubric	4	3	2	1
Focus/Ideas	Clear and focused on important ideas; leaves out unimportant details	Generally clear and focused on important ideas; mostly leaves out unimportant details	Weak focus on important ideas; includes unimportant details	Lack of focus
Organization	Logical, consistent flow of ideas; good transitions	Logical sequencing of ideas; uses transitions	Weak direction and sequenced ideas; some transitions	Lacks structure and transitions
Voice	Engaging, lively; shows writer's personality	Sincere voice connects with reader	Weak voice; little writer involvement	Flat writing with no feeling
Word Choice	Vivid, precise words that bring story to life	Some specific word choice to bring story to life	Limited or repetitive word choice	Vague, dull, or misused words
Sentences	Varied sentence structures	Some variety of sentence structures	Many simple, awkward, or wordy sentences	Run-on sentences, fragments
Conventions	Excellent control and accuracy; *who* and *whom* are used correctly	Good control; few errors; *who* and *whom* generally used correctly	Weak control; *who* and *whom* used incorrectly	Serious errors that obscure meaning

Rubric	6	5	4	3	2	1
Focus/Ideas	Clear, focused review with well-supported opinions	Focused review with mostly well-supported opinions	Some ideas and opinions in review are clear and well supported	Some ideas and opinions in review are clear and well supported	Many ideas and opinions in review are unclear or unsupported	Review lacking clarity and focus
Organization	Organized logically, no gaps; strong central idea	Organized logically, few gaps; fairly strong central idea	Organized somewhat logically; has a clear central idea	Generally organized; has a central idea	Organization not clear; weak topic sentence	Lacking organization; topic sentence weak
Voice	Engaging; shows writer's opinion	Mostly engaging; often shows writer's opinion	Somewhat engaging; sometimes shows writer's opinion	Sometimes flat; writer's opinion not entirely clear	Weak voice; opinion unclear	No identifiable voice
Word Choice	Vivid, precise word choice	Mostly vivid, precise word choice	Accurate word choice	Language lacking accuracy	Limited or repetitive word choice	Poor or limited word choice
Sentences	Varied sentences in logical progression	Generally varied sentences in logical order	Some sentence variety; mostly logical order	Not as much variety; order not always logical	Too many similar sentences; sometimes confusing order	Many sentence fragments and run-ons
Conventions	Excellent control	Good control; few errors	Reasonable control; some errors	Some confusing errors	Little control; many errors	Many serious errors

Rubric	5	4	3	2	1
Focus/Ideas	Clear, focused review with well-supported opinions	Focused review with mostly well-supported opinions	Some ideas and opinions in review are clear and well supported	Many ideas and opinions in review are unclear or unsupported	Review lacking clarity and focus
Organization	Organized logically, no gaps; strong central idea	Organized logically, few gaps; fairly strong central idea	Organized somewhat logically; has a central idea	Organization not clear; weak topic sentence	Lacking organization; topic sentence weak
Voice	Engaging; show writer's opinion	Mostly engaging; sometimes shows writer's opinion	Evident voice connecting with reader	Weak voice; opinion unclear	No identifiable voice
Word Choice	Vivid, precise word choice	Mostly vivid, precise word choice	Accurate word choice	Limited or repetitive word choice	Poor or limited word choice
Sentences	Varied sentences in logical progression	Generally varied sentences in logical order	Not as much variety; mostly logical order	Too many similar sentences	Many sentence fragments and run-ons
Conventions	Excellent control; few or no errors	Good control; some minor errors	Fair control; some errors	Little control; many errors	Many serious errors

Rubric	4	3	2	1
Focus/Ideas	Clear, focused review with well-supported opinions	Most ideas and opinions in review are clear and well supported	Many ideas and opinions in review are unclear or unsupported	Review lacking clarity and focus
Organization	Organized logically, no gaps; strong central idea	Organized logically, few gaps; fairly strong central idea	Organization not clear; weak topic sentence	Lacking organization; topic sentence weak
Voice	Engaging; show writer's opinion	Evident voice connecting with reader	Weak voice; opinion unclear	No identifiable voice
Word Choice	Vivid, precise word choice	Accurate word choice	Limited or repetitive word choice	Poor or limited word choice
Sentences	Varied sentences in logical progression	Not as much variety; mostly logical order	Too many similar sentences	Many sentence fragments and run-ons
Conventions	Excellent control; few or no errors	Good control; few errors	Little control; many errors	Many serious errors

Rubric	6	5	4	3	2	1
Focus/Ideas	Letter with strong supporting details; focused argument	Letter with good details; focused argument	Letter with some good support; reasonable argument	Letter with some supporting details; weak argument	Letter with few supporting details; unclear argument	Letter with no argument or development
Organization	Logical order; argument followed by detailed support	Order mostly logical; main idea, then details	Argument first, then details in generally logical order	Misplaced argument; somewhat disorganized details	Tends to stray; many out of order	Lacks organization
Voice	Formal, persuasive, individual	Persuasive; involved with subject	Mostly persuasive and involved with subject	Somewhat persuasive but not fully involved	Tries to be involved with subject	Not involved with subject
Word Choice	Specific persuasive words	Clear, mostly persuasive words	Generally clear, persuasive words	Few specific or persuasive words	Some vague, repetitive, or incorrect words	Incorrect or limited word choice
Sentences	Structures clear and varied; smooth progression	Good control over sentence structures	Correct sentence structures; some variety	Many simple sentences; little variety	Choppy sentences; lacks variety	Fragments, run-on sentences
Conventions	Excellent control and accuracy	Good control with only minor errors	Reasonable control; some errors	A few serious errors	Errors that may prevent understanding	Frequent errors that affect meaning

Rubric	5	4	3	2	1
Focus/Ideas	Letter with strong supporting details; focused argument	Letter with good details; focused argument	Letter with reasonable argument, some support	Letter with few supporting details; unclear argument	Letter with no argument or development
Organization	Logical order; argument followed by detailed support	Order mostly logical; main idea, then details	Argument first, then details in generally logical order	Tends to stray; some details not in order	Lacks organization
Voice	Formal, persuasive, individual	Persuasive; involved with subject	Mostly persuasive and involved with subject	Trieds to be involved with subject	Not involved with subject
Word Choice	Specific, persuasive words	Clear, mostly persuasive words	Generally clear, persuasive words	Some vague, repetitive, or incorrect words	Incorrect or limited word choice
Sentences	Structures clear and varied; smooth progression	Good control over sentence structures	Correct sentence structures; some variety	Choppy sentences; lacks variety	Fragments, run-on sentences
Conventions	Excellent control and accuracy	Good control with only minor errors	Reasonable control; some errors	Errors that may prevent understanding	Frequent errors that affect meaning

Rubric	4	3	2	1
Focus/Ideas	Letter with strong supporting details; focused argument	Letter with good details; reasonably focused argument	Letter with few supporting details; unclear argument	Letter with no argument or development
Organization	Logical order; argument followed by detailed support	Order mostly logical; main idea, then details	Tends to stray; some details out of order	Lacks organization
Voice	Formal, persuasive, individual	Writer involved with subject	Tries to be involved with subject	Not involved with subject
Word Choice	Specific, persuasive words	Clear, mostly persuasive words	Some vague, repetitive, or incorrect words	Incorrect or limited word choice
Sentences	Structures clear and varied	Control over simple sentence structures	Choppy sentences; lacks variety	Fragment, run-on sentences
Conventions	Excellent control and accuracy	Reasonable control with few errors	Errors that may prevent understanding	Frequent errors that affect meaning

Rubric	6	5	4	3	2	1
Focus/Ideas	Excellent, focused narrative; well elaborated with quality details	Clear, focused narrative; elaborated with appropriate details	Good, focused narrative; adequate elaboration	Good narrative; some elaboration	Sometimes unfocused narrative; needs more supporting details	Rambling narrative; lacks development and detail
Organization	Organized logically; strong beginning, middle, and end	Organized logically; good beginning, middle, and end	Generally logical organization with a beginning, middle, and end	Organization includes a beginning, middle, and end	Organizational pattern attempted, but not clear; little direction from beginning to end	No organizational pattern evident; lacks beginning, middle, and end
Voice	Writer closely involved; engaging personality; lively tone	Writer involved; mostly engaging personality and tone	Pleasant and sincere; somewhat lively tone	Voice mostly pleasant, but not engaging	Little writer involvement, personality; inconsistent tone	Careless writing with no feeling
Word Choice	Many vivid, precise words that bring story to life; excellent use of exaggeration	Some vivid words that bring story to life; good use of exaggeration	Language adequate; occasional use of exaggeration	Language sometimes vague; little or no use of exaggeration	Generally limited or redundant language	Vague, dull, or misused words
Sentences	Excellent variety of sentences; few or no errors	Good variety of sentences; a few minor errors	Sentences mostly complete; some variety	Some sentence errors; little variety	May have simple, awkward, or wordy sentences; lacking variety	Choppy; many incomplete or run-on sentences
Conventions	Excellent control and accuracy; demonstrative adjectives used correctly	Good control, few errors; demonstrative adjectives used correctly	Reasonable control; some errors; most demonstrative adjectives used correctly	Fair control with some serious errors; demonstrative adjectives sometimes used correctly	Weak control; demonstrative adjectives used incorrectly	Serious errors that obscure meaning and prevent understanding

Rubric	5	4	3	2	1
Focus/Ideas	Excellent, focused narrative; well elaborated with quality details	Clear narrative; elaborated with appropriate details	Good, focused narrative; adequate elaboration	Sometimes unfocused narrative; needs more supporting details	Rambling narrative; lacks development and detail
Organization	Organized logically; strong beginning, middle, and end	Organized logically; good beginning, middle, and end	Generally logical organization with a beginning, middle, and end	Organizational pattern attempted, but not clear; little direction from beginning to end	No organizational pattern evident; lacks beginning, middle, and end
Voice	Writer closely involved; engaging personality; lively tone	Writer involved; mostly engaging personality and tone	Pleasant and sincere; somewhat lively tone	Little writer involvement, personality; inconsistent tone	Careless writing with no feeling
Word Choice	Many vivid, precise words that bring story to life; excellent use of exaggeration	Some vivid words that bring story to life; good use of exaggeration	Language adequate; occasional use of exaggeration	Generally limited or redundant language	Vague, dull, or misused words
Sentences	Excellent variety of sentences; few or no errors	Good variety of sentences; a few minor errors	Correctly constructed sentences; some variety	May have simple, awkward, or wordy sentences; little variety	Choppy; many incomplete or run-on sentences
Conventions	Excellent control and accuracy; demonstrative adjectives used correctly	Good control, few errors; demonstrative adjectives used correctly	Reasonable control; some errors; most demonstrative adjectives used correctly	Weak control; demonstrative adjectives used incorrectly	Serious errors that obscure meaning and prevent understanding

Rubric	4	3	2	1
Focus/Ideas	Excellent, focused narrative; well elaborated with quality details	Good, focused narrative; adequate elaboration	Sometimes unfocused narrative; needs more supporting details	Rambling narrative; lacks development and detail
Organization	Organized logically; strong beginning, middle, and end	Organized logically; good beginning, middle, and end	Organizational pattern attempted, but not clear; little direction from beginning to end	No organizational pattern evident; lacks beginning, middle, and end
Voice	Writer closely involved; engaging personality; lively tone	Pleasant and sincere; somewhat lively tone	Little writer involvement, personality; inconsistent tone	Careless writing with no feeling
Word Choice	Vivid precise words that bring story to life; excellent use of exaggeration	Language adequate; occasional use of exaggeration	Generally limited or redundant language, little use of exaggeration	Vague or misused words, no exaggeration
Sentences	Excellent variety of sentences; few or no errors	Correctly constructed sentences; some variety	May have simple, awkward, or wordy sentences; little variety	Choppy; many incomplete or run-on sentences
Conventions	Excellent control and accuracy; demonstrative adjectives used correctly	Good control, few errors; demonstrative adjectives generally used correctly	Weak control; demonstrative adjectives used incorrectly	Serious errors that obscure meaning and prevent understanding

Rubric	6	5	4	3	2	1
Focus/Ideas	Gives clear, specific information about events, exhibits, and ideas; uses appropriate details	Gives specific information about events, exhibits, and ideas; uses some details	Gives accurate information about events, exhibits, and ideas with a few details	Gives information about events, exhibits, and ideas; limited detail	Gives limited or unclear information about events, exhibits, and ideas; few or no details	Brochure with no clarity or development
Organization	Organized logically	Organized logically with few gaps	Organized somewhat logically with some gaps	Organization is generally clear but has gaps	Organizational pattern attempted, but not clear	No organizational pattern evident
Voice	Engaging, lovely, and persuasive	Mostly engaging with persuasive tone	Generally engaging with persuasive tone	Evident voice with some persuasion	Weak voice; no persuasive tone	Flat writing with no identifiable voice
Word Choice	Informative, vivid, precise words	Informative and appropriate word choice	Generally appropriate word choice	Unspecific word choice provides little information or detail	Limited or dull word choice	Dull and ineffective
Sentences	Varied sentence types that sustain interest	Mostly varied sentence types that flow well	Sentences somewhat varied with reasonable flow	Little variety; many simple sentences	Too many similar sentences; choppy	Run-on sentences, fragments
Conventions	Excellent control and accuracy; comparative and superlative adjectives used correctly	Good control, few errors; comparative and superlative adjectives generally used correctly	Reasonable control; comparative and superlative adjectives sometimes used correctly	Numerous errors, most minor; comparative and superlative adjectives mostly used incorrectly	Weak control; comparative and superlative adjectives used incorrectly	Serious errors that obscure meaning

Rubric	5	4	3	2	1
Focus/Ideas	Gives clear, specific information about events, exhibits, and ideas; uses appropriate details	Gives specific information about events, exhibits, and ideas; uses some details	Gives information about events, exhibits, and ideas with some detail	Gives limited or unclear information about events, exhibits, and ideas; limited detail	Brochure with no clarity or development
Organization	Organized logically	Organized logically with few gaps	Organization is generally clear	Organizational pattern attempted, but not clear	No organizational pattern evident
Voice	Engaging, lovely, and persuasive	Mostly engaging with persuasive tone	Evident voice with some persuasion	Weak voice; no persuasive tone	Flat writing with no identifiable voice
Word Choice	Informative, vivid, precise words	Informative and appropriate word choice	Some specific word choice to provide information and detail	Limited or dull word choice	Dull and ineffective
Sentences	Varied sentence types that sustain interest	Mostly varied sentence types that flow well	Some variety in sentence types; many simple sentences	Too many similar sentences; choppy	Run-on sentences, fragments
Conventions	Excellent control and accuracy; comparative and superlative adjectives used correctly	Good control, few errors; comparative and superlative adjectives generally used correctly	Reasonable control, some minor errors; comparative and superlative adjectives sometimes used correctly	Weak control; comparative and superlative adjectives used incorrectly	Serious errors that obscure meaning

Rubric	4	3	2	1
Focus/Ideas	Gives specific information about events, exhibits, and ideas; uses details	Gives information about events, exhibits, and ideas with some detail	Gives limited or unclear information about events, exhibits, and ideas; limited detail	Brochure with no clarity or development
Organization	Organized logically	Organized logically with few gaps	Organizational pattern attempted, but not clear	No organizational pattern evident
Voice	Engaging, lovely, and persuasive	Evident voice with some persuasion	Weak voice; no persuasive tone	Flat writing with no identifiable voice
Word Choice	Informative, vivid, precise words	Some specific word choice to provide information and detail	Limited or dull word choice	Dull and ineffective
Sentences	Varied sentence types that sustain interest	Some variety in sentence types; many simple sentences	Too many similar sentences; choppy	Run-on sentences, fragments
Conventions	Excellent control and accuracy; comparative and superlative adjectives used correctly	Good control, few errors; comparative and superlative adjectives generally used correctly	Weak control; comparative and superlative adjectives used incorrectly	Serious errors that obscure meaning

Rubric	6	5	4	3	2	1
Focus/Ideas	Clear, focused essay with identifiable causes and effects and many strong supporting details	Clear essay with identifiable causes and effects and good supporting details	Most ideas, including causes and effects, are clear and supported	Some ideas, including causes and effects, are supported	Many ideas, including causes and effects, are unclear or off topic	Essay with no development, clear causes or effects
Organization	Organized logically, no gaps; strong topic sentence	Organized logically, few gaps; clear topic sentence	Organized somewhat logically, some gaps; adequate topic sentence	Organization sometimes unclear; weak topic sentence	Organizational pattern attempted but not clear; unclear topic sentence	No organizational pattern evident; no topic sentence
Voice	Engaging, clear, and logical	Clear and logical; generally engaging	Generally clear and logical; somewhat engaging	Uneven effort at clarity or logic; voice somewhat flat	Weak voice	Flat writing with no identifiable voice
Word Choice	Vivid, precise word choice; strong use of cause-and-effect clue words	Vivid word choice with good use of cause-and-effect clue words	Accurate word choice with fair use of cause-and-effect clue words	Often vague word choice with little or no use of cause-and-effect clue words	Limited or repetitive word choice and use of clue words	Incorrect, limited word choice with no cause-and-effect clue words
Sentences	Varied sentences in logical progression	Generally varied sentences in logical progression	Some sentence variation; mostly logical progression	Not as much variety; order sometimes confusing	Too many similar sentences	Many fragments and run-ons
Conventions	Excellent control and accuracy; adverbs used correctly	Good control, few errors; adverbs generally used correctly	Reasonable control, mostly minor errors; adverbs sometimes used incorrectly	Reasonable control, some serious errors; adverbs often used incorrectly	Weak control; no adverbs	Serious errors that obscure meaning

Rubric	5	4	3	2	1
Focus/Ideas	Clear, focused essay with identifiable causes and effects and many strong supporting details	Clear essay with identifiable causes and effects and good supporting details	Most ideas, including causes and effects, are clear and supported	Some ideas, including causes and effects, are unclear or off topic	Essay with no development, clear causes or effects
Organization	Organized logically, no gaps; strong topic sentence	Organized logically, few gaps; clear topic sentence	Organized somewhat logically, some gaps; adequate topic sentence	Organizational pattern attempted but not clear; weak topic sentence	No organizational pattern evident; topic sentence
Voice	Engaging, clear, and logical	Clear and logical; somewhat engaging	Evident voice connecting with reader	Weak voice	Flat writing with no identifiable voice
Word Choice	Vivid, precise word choice; strong use of cause-and-effect clue words	Vivid word choice with good use of cause-and-effect clue words	Accurate word choice with fair use of cause-and-effect clue words	Limited or repetitive word choice and use of clue words	Incorrect, limited word choice with no cause-and-effect clue words
Sentences	Varied sentences in logical progression	Generally varied sentences in understandable progression	Not as much variety; order mostly logical	Too many similar sentences	Many fragments and run-ons
Conventions	Excellent control and accuracy; adverbs used correctly	Good control, few errors; adverbs generally used correctly	Reasonable control, some serious errors; adverbs sometimes used incorrectly	Weak control; adverbs used incorrectly	Serious errors that obscure meaning

Rubric	4	3	2	1
Focus/Ideas	Clear, focused essay with identifiable causes and effects and many supporting details	Most ideas, including causes and effects, are clear and supported	Some ideas, including causes and effects, are unclear or off topic	Essay with no development, clear causes or effects
Organization	Organized logically, no gaps; strong topic sentence	Organized logically, few gaps; fairly strong topic sentence	Organizational pattern attempted but not clear; weak topic sentence	No organizational pattern evident; topic sentence
Voice	Engaging; shows writer's feelings about subject	Evident voice connecting with reader	Weak voice	Flat writing with no identifiable voice
Word Choice	Vivid, precise word choice with strong use of cause-and-effect clue words	Accurate word choice with good use of cause-and-effect clue words	Limited or repetitive word choice and use of clue words	Incorrect, limited word choice with no cause-and-effect clue words
Sentences	Varied sentences in logical progression	Not as much variety; order mostly logical	Too many similar sentences	Many fragments and run-ons
Conventions	Excellent control and accuracy; adverbs used correctly	Good control, few errors; adverbs generally used correctly	Weak control; adverbs used incorrectly	Serious errors that obscure meaning

Rubric	6	5	4	3	2	1
Focus/Ideas	Excellent, focused narrative; well elaborated with vivid sensory details	Strongly focused narrative; elaborated with vivid sensory details	Generally focused narrative; elaborated with some sensory details	Sometimes unfocused narrative; needs more compelling detail	Often unfocused narrative; needs a lot more detail	Rambling narrative; lacks development and detail
Organization	Organized logically; strong characters and plot that mirror the parody's original	Organization is mostly logical; characters and plot mirror the parody's original	Coherent beginning, middle, and end; good tie-ins to the parody's original	Little direction from beginning to end; few or weak tie-ins to the parody's original	Almost no direction from beginning to end; few and weak tie-ins to parody's original	Lacks beginning, middle, or end; few or no clear ties to parody's original
Voice	Voice closely imitates original; adds new twists	Voice closely imitates original with new twists	Voice imitates original with new twists	Voice has weak connection to original; few or no twists	Voice has almost no connection to original; almost no twists	Voice has no connection to original
Word Choice	Vivid language—borrowed and new; distinct language of the parody's source	Some vivid language—borrowed and new; too much or too little language from parody's source	Clear words to bring story to life; too much or too little language from parody's source.	Generally limited or repetitive word choice; not much language from parody's source	Limited or repetitive word choice; almost no language from parody's source	Incorrect or very limited word choice; no connection to style of the original.
Sentences	Excellent variety of sentences; natural rhythm	Strong variety of sentences; mostly natural rhythm	Correctly constructed sentences; some variety	Some simple, awkward, or wordy sentences; some variety	Many simple, awkward, or wordy sentences; little variety	Choppy; many incomplete or run-on sentences
Conventions	Excellent control; modifiers used vividly and correctly	Strong control; modifiers used correctly, often vividly	No serious errors to affect understanding; modifiers generally used correctly	Weak control; several modifiers used incorrectly	Very little control; modifiers used incorrectly almost every time	Many errors that prevent understanding

Rubric	5	4	3	2	1
Focus/Ideas	Excellent, focused narrative; well elaborated with vivid sensory details	Generally focused narrative; elaborated with some sensory details	Sometimes unfocused narrative; needs more compelling detail	Often unfocused narrative; needs a lot more detail	Rambling narrative; lacks development and detail
Organization	Organized logically; strong characters and plot that mirror the parody's original	Coherent beginning, middle, and end; good tie-ins to the parody's original	Little direction from beginning to end; few or weak tie-ins to the parody's original	Almost no direction from beginning to end; few and weak tie-ins to parody's original	Lacks beginning, middle, or end; few or no clear ties to parody's original
Voice	Voice closely imitates original; adds new twists	Voice imitates original with new twists	Voice has weak connection to original; few or no twists	Voice has almost no connection to original; almost no twists	Voice has no connection to original
Word Choice	Vivid language—borrowed and new. Distinct language of the parody's source	Clear words to bring story to life. Too much or too little language from parody's source.	Generally limited or repetitive word choice; not much language from parody's source	Limited or repetitive word choice; almost no language from parody's source	Incorrect or very limited word choice; no connection to style of the original.
Sentences	Excellent variety of sentences; natural rhythm	Correctly constructed sentences; some variety	Some simple, awkward, or wordy sentences; little variety	Many simple, awkward, or wordy sentences; close to no variety	Choppy; many incomplete or run-on sentences
Conventions	Excellent control; modifiers used vividly and correctly	No serious errors to affect understanding; modifiers generally used correctly	Weak control; several modifiers used incorrectly	Very little control; modifiers used incorrectly almost every time	Many errors that prevent understanding

Rubric	4	3	2	1
Focus/Ideas	Excellent, focused narrative; well elaborated with vivid sensory details	Generally focused narrative; elaborated with some sensory details	Sometimes unfocused narrative; needs more compelling detail	Rambling narrative; lacks development and detail
Organization	Organized logically; strong characters and plot that mirror the parody's original	Coherent beginning, middle, and end; good tie-ins to the parody's original	Little direction from beginning to end; few or weak tie-ins to the parody's original	Lacks beginning, middle, or end; few or no clear ties to parody's original
Voice	Voice closely imitates original; adds new twists	Voice imitates original with new twists	Voice has weak connection to original; few or no twists	Voice has no connection to original
Word Choice	Vivid language—borrowed and new. Distinct language of the parody's source	Clear words to bring story to life. Too much or too little language from parody's source.	Generally limited or repetitive word choice; not much language from parody's source	Incorrect or very limited word choice. No connection to style of the original.
Sentences	Excellent variety of sentences; natural rhythm	Correctly constructed sentences; some variety	Some simple, awkward, or wordy sentences; little variety	Choppy; many incomplete or run-on sentences
Conventions	Excellent control; modifiers used vividly and correctly	No serious errors to affect understanding; modifiers generally used correctly	Weak control; several modifiers used incorrectly	Many errors that prevent understanding

Rubric	6	5	4	3	2	1
Focus/Ideas	Clear, focused topics with appropriate details	Most topics clear; most details appropriate	Some topics clear; some details inappropriate	Some topics unclear, off subject; extraneous details	Most topics unclear, off subject; few pertinent details	No clarity of topics or important details
Organization	Organized logically, no gaps	Organized logically, few gaps	Organization is mostly logical; a few gaps	Organizational pattern attempted, somewhat clear	Organizational pattern attempted, not clear	No organizational pattern evident
Voice	Writer has clearly paraphrased; no plagiarism	Writer has paraphrased; no evidence of plagiarism	Writer has copied a few words; possible plagiarism	Writer has copied some of author's words; likely plagiarism	Writer copied many of the author's words; evident plagiarism	Writer copied words exactly; clear plagiarism
Word Choice	Notes accurately paraphrased throughout	Notes accurately paraphrased in most places	Notes accurately paraphrased in some places	Few notes paraphrased	One or two notes paraphrased	None of the notes paraphrased
Sentences	Notes include citations	Most information in notes is cited	Some of the information in notes is cited	Most of the information in notes is not cited	Only one or two citations	No information is cited
Conventions	Excellent control and accuracy; conjunctions used correctly	Good control, few errors; conjunctions generally used correctly	Adequate control, many errors; conjunctions frequently incorrect	Weak control; conjunctions used incorrectly	Almost no control; conjunctions used incorrectly	Serious errors that obscure meaning

Rubric	5	4	3	2	1
Focus/Ideas	Clear, focused topics with appropriate details	Most topics clear; most details appropriate	Some topics clear; some details inappropriate	Some topics unclear, off subject; extraneous details	No clarity of topics or important details
Organization	Organized logically, no gaps	Organized logically, few gaps	Organization is mostly logical; a few gaps	Organizational pattern attempted, but not clear	No organizational pattern evident
Voice	Writer has clearly paraphrased; no plagiarism	Writer has paraphrased; no evidence of plagiarism	Writer has copied some of author's words; likely plagiarism	Writer copied many of author's words; evident plagiarism	Writer copied words exactly; clear plagiarism
Word Choice	Notes accurately paraphrased throughout	Notes accurately paraphrased in most places	Notes accurately paraphrased in some places	Few notes paraphrased	None of the notes paraphrased
Sentences	Notes include citations	Most information in notes is cited	Most of the information in notes is not cited	Only one or two citations	No information is cited
Conventions	Excellent control and accuracy; conjunctions used correctly	Good control, few errors; conjunctions generally used correctly	Adequate control, many errors; conjunctions frequently incorrect	Weak control; conjunctions used incorrectly	Serious errors that obscure meaning

Rubric	4	3	2	1
Focus/Ideas	Clear, focused topics with appropriate details	Most topics clear; most details appropriate	Some topics unclear, off subject; extraneous details	No clarity of topics or important details
Organization	Organized logically, no gaps	Organized logically, few gaps	Organizational pattern attempted, but not clear	No organizational pattern evident
Voice	Writer has clearly paraphrased; no plagiarism	Writer has mostly paraphrased; possible plagiarism	Writer has copied most of author's words; likely plagiarism	Writer copied words exactly; clear plagiarism
Word Choice	Notes accurately paraphrased throughout	Notes accurately paraphrased in most places	Few notes paraphrased	None of the notes paraphrased
Sentences	Notes include citations	Most information in notes is cited	Most of the information in notes is not cited	No information is cited
Conventions	Excellent control and accuracy; conjunctions used correctly	Good control, few errors; conjunctions generally used correctly	Weak control; conjunctions used incorrectly	Serious errors that obscure meaning

Rubric	6	5	4	3	2	1
Focus/Ideas	Clearly stated with several details as well as descriptive and/or persuasive language	Clearly stated with at least one detail; descriptive language	Stated with at least one detail	Stated, but not supported	Stated but unclear; barely supported	Not stated; no supporting details
Organization	Organized logically; strong introductory sentence	Organized logically; fairly strong introductory sentence	Organization is mostly logical; adequate introductory sentence	Organization pattern attempted but not clear; weak topic sentence	Little organization pattern evident; topic sentence is weak or nonexistent	No organizational pattern evident; topic sentence weak or nonexistent
Voice	Engaging; persuasive	Evident voice appealing to reader	Voice is sometimes not evident; occasionally appealing to reader	Weak voice	Very weak voice, or no identifiable voice	Flat writing with no identifiable voice
Word Choice	Precise word choice; concise	Accurate word choice	Generally accurate word choice	Adequate word choice	Limited or repetitive word choice	Incorrect or very limited word choice
Sentences	Excellent awareness of audience	Good awareness of audience	Adequate awareness of audience	Ambiguous awareness of audience	Almost no awareness of audience	No awareness of audience
Conventions	Excellent control and clarity; commas used correctly	Good control; commas generally used correctly	Adequate control; commas sometimes used correctly	Weak control; commas used incorrectly	Almost no control; many serious errors	Serious errors that obscure meaning

Rubric	5	4	3	2	1
Focus/Ideas	Clearly stated with several details as well as descriptive and/or persuasive language	Clearly stated with at least one detail; descriptive language	Stated with at least one detail	Stated, but not supported	Not stated; no supporting details
Organization	Organized logically; strong introductory sentence	Organized logically; fairly strong introductory sentence	Organization is mostly logical; adequate introductory sentence	Organization pattern attempted but not clear; weak topic sentence	No organizational pattern evident; topic sentence weak or nonexistent
Voice	Engaging; persuasive	Evident voice appealing to reader	Voice is sometimes not evident; occasionally appealing to reader	Weak voice	Flat writing with no identifiable voice
Word Choice	Precise word choice; concise	Accurate word choice	Sometimes accurate word choice; often limited or repetitive	Limited or repetitive word choice	Incorrect or very limited word choice
Sentences	Excellent awareness of audience	Good awareness of audience	Adequate awareness of audience	Ambiguous awareness of audience	No awareness of audience
Conventions	Excellent control and clarity; commas used correctly	Good control; commas generally used correctly	Adequate control; commas sometimes used correctly	Weak control; commas used incorrectly	Serious errors that obscure meaning

Rubric	4	3	2	1
Focus/Ideas	Clearly stated with several details as well as descriptive and/or persuasive language	Clearly stated with at least one detail; descriptive language	Stated, but not supported	Not stated; no supporting details
Organization	Organized logically; strong introductory sentence	Organized logically; fairly strong introductory sentence	Organization pattern attempted but not clear; weak topic sentence	No organizational pattern evident; topic sentence weak or nonexistent
Voice	Engaging; persuasive	Evident voice appealing to reader	Weak voice	Flat writing with no identifiable voice
Word Choice	Precise word choice; concise	Accurate word choice	Limited or repetitive word choice	Incorrect or very limited word choice
Sentences	Excellent awareness of audience	Good awareness of audience	Ambiguous awareness of audience	No awareness of audience
Conventions	Excellent control and clarity; commas used correctly	Good control, few errors; commas generally used correctly	Weak control; commas used incorrectly	Serious errors that obscure meaning

Rubric	6	5	4	3	2	1
Focus/Ideas	Excellent, focused narrative; well elaborated with quality details	Tightly focused narrative; elaborated with quality details	Narrative focused; elaborated with some details	Sometimes focused; needs more supporting details	Frequently unfocused; needs many more supporting details	Rambling narrative; lacks development and detail
Organization	Logical, consistent flow of ideas; good transitions	Mostly logical, consistent flow of ideas; several good transitions	Logical sequence with some transitions	Little direction from beginning to end; few order words	Almost no direction from beginning to end; few order words	Lacks structure and transitions
Voice	Engaging; shows author's involvement	Mostly engaging; shows author's involvement	Reveals personality	Little writer involvement, personality	Almost no writer involvement; little feeling	Careless writing with no feeling
Word Choice	Vivid, precise words that bring story to life	Several vivid, precise words that bring story to life	Clear word choice that brings story to life	Limited or repetitive word choice	Limited and repetitive word choice; some vague or misused words	Vague, dull, or misused words
Sentences	Varied sentences in logical progression	Strong variety of sentences in mostly logical progression	Not as much variety; order logical	Too many similar sentences	Many similar sentences; a few fragments and run-ons	Many fragments and run-on sentences
Conventions	Excellent control; no errors in the use of quotation marks	Strong control; one or two errors in the use of quotation marks	Good control, most quotation marks placed correctly	Weak control; some quotation marks placed incorrectly	Almost no control; many quotation marks placed incorrectly	Many errors that seriously detract from writing

Rubric	5	4	3	2	1
Focus/Ideas	Excellent, focused narrative; well elaborated with quality details	Narrative focused; elaborated with some details	Sometimes focused; needs more supporting details	Frequently unfocused; needs many more supporting details	Rambling narrative; lacks development and detail
Organization	Logical, consistent flow of ideas; good transitions	Logical sequence with some transitions	Little direction from beginning to end; few order words	Almost no direction from beginning to end; few order words	Lacks structure and transitions
Voice	Engaging; shows author's involvement	Reveals personality	Little writer involvement, personality	Almost no writer involvement; little feeling	Careless writing with no feeling
Word Choice	Vivid, precise words that bring story to life	Clear word choice that brings story to life	Limited or repetitive word choice	Limited and repetitive word choice; some vague or misused words	Vague, dull, or misused words
Sentences	Varied sentences in logical progression	Not as much variety; order logical	Too many similar sentences	Many similar sentences; a few fragments and run-ons	Many fragments and run-on sentences
Conventions	Excellent control; no errors in the use of quotation marks	Good control, most quotation marks placed correctly	Weak control; some quotation marks placed incorrectly	Almost no control; many quotation marks placed incorrectly	Many errors that seriously detract from writing

Rubric	4	3	2	1
Focus/Ideas	Excellent, focused narrative; well elaborated with quality details	Narrative focused; elaborated with some details	Sometimes focused; needs more supporting details	Rambling narrative; lacks development and detail
Organization	Logical, consistent flow of ideas; good transitions	Logical sequence with some transitions	Little direction from beginning to end; few order words	Lacks structure and transitions
Voice	Engaging; shows author's involvement	Reveals personality	Little writer involvement, personality	Careless writing with no feeling
Word Choice	Vivid, precise words that bring story to life	Clear word choice that brings story to life	Limited or repetitive word choice	Vague, dull, or misused words
Sentences	Varied sentences in logical progression	Not as much variety; order logical	Too many similar sentences	Many fragments and run-on sentences
Conventions	Excellent control; no errors in the use of quotation marks	Good control, most quotation marks placed correctly	Weak control; some quotation marks placed incorrectly	Many errors that seriously detract from writing

Rubric	6	5	4	3	2	1
Focus/Ideas	Clear, focused essay addresses the prompt	Clear essay, but gives too much or too little information	Sometimes vague essay; addresses the prompt	Vague essay that weakly addresses the prompt	Extremely vague essay; weakly addresses the prompt	Rambling essay; lacks development and detail
Organization	Logical organization; good transitions and details	Some sequenced ideas with some transitions	A few sequenced ideas; adequate use of order words	Some details; few order words	Almost no details; one or two order words	Lacks structure and transitions
Voice	Engaging, lively, and enthusiastic writing	Language correct, but shows little personality	Language sometimes incorrect; little personality	Little originality, personality, or involvement	Almost no originality, personality, or involvement	Careless writing with no feeling
Word Choice	Specific, persuasive words highlight qualifications	Some persuasive words to express ideas	A few persuasive words to express ideas; sometimes limited language	Generally limited or redundant language	Mostly limited or redundant language; some misused words	Vague, dull, or misused words
Sentences	Varied and clear sentence structure	Some sentence variety and length	Not enough sentence variety and length; a couple of wordy or awkward sentences	Some wordy or awkward sentences; little variety	Many wordy or awkward sentences; very little variety	Choppy; many incomplete or run-on sentences
Conventions	Excellent control; few or no errors	Good control; few errors	Occasionally weak control; a few errors	Weak control; many errors	A few serious errors that hamper understanding	Many serious errors that prevent understanding

Rubric	5	4	3	2	1
Focus/Ideas	Clear, focused essay addresses the prompt	Clear essay, but gives too much or too little information	Sometimes vague essay; addresses the prompt	Vague essay that weakly addresses the prompt	Rambling essay; lacks development and detail
Organization	Logical organization; good transitions and details	Some sequenced ideas with some transitions	A few sequenced ideas; adequate use of order words	Some details; few order words	Lacks structure and transitions
Voice	Engaging, lively, and enthusiastic writing	Language correct, but shows little personality	Language sometimes incorrect; little personality	Little originality, personality, or involvement	Careless writing with no feeling
Word Choice	Specific, persuasive words highlight qualifications	Some persuasive words to express ideas	A few persuasive words to express ideas; sometimes limited language	Generally limited or redundant language	Vague, dull, or misused words
Sentences	Varied and clear sentence structure	Some sentence variety and length	Not enough sentence variety and length; a couple of wordy or awkward sentences	Some wordy or awkward sentences; little variety	Choppy; many incomplete or run-on sentences
Conventions	Excellent control; few or no errors	Good control; few errors	Occasionally weak control; some errors	Weak control; many errors	Many serious errors that prevent understanding

Rubric	4	3	2	1
Focus/Ideas	Clear, focused essay addresses the prompt	Clear essay, but gives too much or too little information	Vague essay that weakly addresses the prompt	Rambling essay; lacks development and detail
Organization	Logical organization; good transitions and details	Some sequenced ideas with some transitions	Some details; few order words	Lacks structure and transitions
Voice	Engaging, lively, and enthusiastic writing	Language correct, but shows little personality	Little originality, personality, or involvement	Careless writing with no feeling
Word Choice	Specific, persuasive words highlight qualifications	Some persuasive words to express ideas	Generally limited or redundant language	Vague, dull, or misused words
Sentences	Varied and clear sentence structure	Some sentence variety and length	Some wordy or awkward sentences; little variety	Choppy; many incomplete or run-on sentences
Conventions	Excellent control; few or no errors	Good control; few errors	Weak control; many errors	Many serious errors that prevent understanding